QUESTIONS
FOR TODAY

QUESTIONS FOR TODAY

by

EDWARD H. PATEY

Dean Emeritus of Liverpool Cathedral

MOWBRAY
LONDON & OXFORD

Copyright © Edward H. Patey 1986

ISBN 0 264 66848 0

First published 1986 by A. R. Mowbray & Co. Ltd,
Saint Thomas House, Becket Street, Oxford, OX1 1SJ

Typeset by Cotswold Typesetting Ltd, Cheltenham
Printed in Great Britain by Cox & Wyman Ltd, Reading

British Library Cataloguing in Publication Data

Patey, Edward H.
  Questions for today.—(Mowbray's popular
  Christian paperbacks)
  1. Christian life
  I. Title
  248.4   BV4501.2

ISBN 0-264-66848-0

CONTENTS

ACKNOWLEDGEMENTS

The author of a book which attempts to cover a wide range of contemporary questions within a short space must depend on the researches and opinions of men and women more knowledgeable than himself. Much of this debt cannot be acknowledged. But gratitude can be expressed to a number of individuals who have provided valuable material or allowed me to quote from their works.

These include:

Canon G. B. Bentley; the Bishop of Birmingham; Professor D. K. Britton; Prebendary John Gladwin; the Revd Robert Nind; the Revd Dr Stephen Orchard; Canon Paul Oestreicher; Dr D. W. B. Sainsbury; Mrs Margaret Simey; Sir Ralph Verney.

The following publishers have generously given permission for the inclusion of copyright material: The Commission for Racial Equality; The National Council for Civil Liberties; The Student Christian Movement Press (*God Among Us*); Macdonald and Evans (*Policing Freedom*) and the Legal Board of the General Synod (*Human Fertilisation and Embryology. Homosexual Relationships. Faith in the City*).

The biblical quotations are from the New English Bible, © 1970, The Oxford and Cambridge University Presses.

E.H.P.

INTRODUCTION

Taking Questions Seriously

In October 1985 the Oxford Union Society invited Mrs Victoria Gillick to take part in a debate with Dr Germaine Greer on the controversial question whether doctors should be permitted to give birth control advice to girls under sixteen without the knowledge and consent of their parents. Mrs Gillick had a few days previously lost her appeal in the House of Lords to have such advice declared illegal. Her visit to Oxford so soon after the judgement had been made public attracted considerable interest among members of the University. In the debating hall every seat was taken. But the occasion was marred by the action of a group of student protestors who attempted to block her way into the chamber in the hope of preventing her from speaking. Scuffles broke out, there were mutual accusations of violence, and the police had to be called to restore order.

A few weeks later a Home Office Minister, Mr David Waddington, was greeted with spitting, jeering and jostling when he entered a hall in Manchester University to address a student meeting on the Government's immigration policy. He was unable to make himself heard, and the meeting had to be abandoned. Nor is it only university students who have fallen victim to this fashion of trying to deny a hearing to those who think differently. On more than one occasion at the 1985 Trades Union Congress a 'comrade' trying to put his case at the rostrum was shouted down by other 'comrades' in the hall with the chairman vainly trying to restore order.

The saying attributed to Voltaire: 'I disapprove of what you say but will defend to the death your right to say it' is thought by many today to be a sign of weakness. The popular politics of confrontation usually indicates an unwillingness to take seriously any point of view except one's own. This is a trivial way of trying to find answers to serious questions. For every argument has at least two sides to it, generally many more. These need to be understood and carefully considered before a final answer can be reached. All the issues discussed in this book are difficult and controversial. Contrasting views are strongly held on each one of them. It would be easier for the reader (and for the author) to come down firmly on one side of each question, and to dismiss all contradictory arguments as unworthy of consideration. But that is not the way to reach the truth. Nor is it the purpose of this book which is to encourage further thought on the matters raised, rather than to provide easy answers.

Questions with easy answers are generally not worth asking. None of the questions discussed in this book is easy. For many of them there is no clear answer. Yet each one is of great personal concern to us all, and the happiness and well-being of our families, local communities, nation and the world itself depends on the kind of answers we try to give. These questions are to do with the relationships between the sexes, marriage and family life. They are to do with the impact of scientific research and medical technology on matters concerning the beginning of life and the approach of death. They are to do with the maintenance of law and order at a time of increased violence in our streets and on the football terraces, of terrorism and outrage on a world scale, and of the new demands which the present situation places upon the police and the courts. They are to do with the tragedy of unemployment and the revolution in the familiar pattern of work and leisure which faces us as computers and robots begin to do the jobs which once occupied many pairs of hands. They are to do with the violation of the countryside with the coming of modern sophisticated agricultural technology, the consequent scarcity of many birds, insects and plants once commonly seen, and with the growing anxiety felt by the public about factory farming. They are to do also with the place of the Christian faith and the role of the Church in providing the moral basis without which these questions cannot be adequately examined. These are all down-to-earth questions which feature day by day on our television screens and in the daily press. But society is deeply divided on the solutions to these problems, and Christians share in these divisions. Other questions, such as those which concern war and peace, addiction, or poverty are equally pressing, but are beyond the scope of this present book.

This book attempts to examine these questions for today in the light of the Christian faith. It would be comforting to be able to claim that the followers of Jesus Christ were able to agree on clear and unanimous answers to them all. But this is not so. Nor should it surprise us. It is easy enough to read the Ten Commandments and hear the divine command to keep the Sabbath day holy, to refrain from murder, adultery and theft, to avoid covetousness. So far, so good. But as soon as we try to apply these general injunctions to the specific moral problems which face us, the guidance becomes less clear. Does the fourth commandment mean that it is a sin to watch television on Sunday, or buy a newspaper, or fill up the car at a petrol station? Has the seventh commandment any guidance to give on divorce or remarriage? Does the eighth commandment condemn gambling on football pools or even (as some would have it) speculation on the stock exchange? Is the tenth commandment a condemnation of advertisements (such as we see on television) which are designed to stimulate greed and envy, or the credit cards which claim to 'take the waiting out of wanting'? Good church people with the Ten Commandments in their hands will come to many different conclusions about their meaning in practical terms for today. They can search the rest of the Bible and quote texts to justify a wide variety of different solutions to contemporary moral problems. It is not only individual Christians who come to different conclusions in spite of claiming the same faith. In the course of history the Churches have developed differing and characteristic stances on such matters as birth control, divorce, gambling, alcohol and war. Nor can we expect the Bible or the dogmas of the Church to provide quick answers to the many new ethical problems we have to face today, such as those raised by the Warnock Report. The truth is that we must not expect to find easy answers to complex questions in the traditional documents of our religion, though both Bible and Church teaching remain essential tools in our quest. Christians who claim to have found in the Bible or traditional theology clear-cut and absolute answers to all our contemporary problems may be envied for their certainty, but not necessarily believed. Their convictions may come from a desire (conscious or unconscious) to dodge the real issues by resorting to a naïve over-simplification.

Those who want absolute answers will not find them in the following pages. Instead, readers are invited to set out on a more adventurous journey. As a first step, they are asked to take the relevant facts behind the questions with great seriousness. Immediately on the publication of the Warnock Report on Human Fertilisation worshippers in some churches were invited to sign petitions opposing its recommendations. It is obvious that those who added their signatures were well-intentioned people who had not themselves read the report nor had had the opportunity of considering its highly technical implications. Every subject discussed in this book has been the object of long and painstaking research and investigation by bodies of experts and informed individuals. Even after this, opinion is divided. Christians have a duty to face facts and treat them with respect. It is no part of a Christian's response to ignore one half of the argument in order to come to a snap judgement. The material presented in these chapters does not claim to be more than a brief introduction to the relevant facts. A list of books and of other sources of information is given at the end of each chapter for those who wish to explore the subjects further. Those using this book for group study do well to invite local experts to join them to provide more background material to help in their deliberations.

Having examined the facts, the next task is to consider what aspects of the Bible or Church teaching are likely to be relevant to the matter in hand. Each chapter includes a number of Biblical references which should be carefully studied. Many of the problems discussed in this book have attracted the attention of religious pressure groups which have a particular point of view to promote. They usually emanate from the more extreme 'high' or 'low' wings of Church opinion. If their material comes to hand, it should be carefully and critically studied, bearing in mind the particular source from which they come. Their arguments may eventually convince you, but initially it is sensible to treat them with caution.

Obviously the writer of this book also has his own point of view, strongly held on many of these issues. Percipient readers may be made aware of this from time to time. But this is not intended to be a work of propaganda but the starting point of a journey of thought and discussion which may lead those who take it in a number of different directions. In every chapter the various positions held by Christians of equal sincerity are noted. Those who use this book for group study are likely to encounter this same diversity. This should not cause any anxiety. This is not an examination paper in which all candidates are expected to produce the same answers! Differences of opinion within the Church may be a hopeful sign that people are honestly struggling to find the answers for themselves and not taking the soft option of latching on to texts or slogans in the hope of finding an easy short cut.

We must use all our God-given faculties to try to apply the faith we profess towards a solution of these bewildering questions for today. But how? If evidently neither the Bible nor the Church is able to give instant solutions to all our problems, where do we look for help? The answer is—we must look to Jesus Christ. In Jesus we can see the one man in human history who lived a life in complete communion with God. His response to every situation he met and every individual he encountered was totally in tune with the divine purpose. By taking pains to become closely acquainted with all the Bible tells us about Jesus—his teaching, his parables, his miracles and his style of life—we can begin to build up a picture of what Paul called 'the mind of Christ'. We do not find in his teaching detailed instructions on how to deal with the problems of test-tube babies or the use of pesticides or unemployment, but we can grow in our understanding of him in such a way that we begin to find ourselves asking the questions he would certainly want us to ask and to search for the answers which are in tune with his teaching and character. So our thinking and our consciences begin to be tuned to harmonize with the model which Jesus gives, and we begin to find ourselves applauding one course of action and opposing another because our Christian intuition compels us to do so. We may discover, as this book illustrates, that fellow Christians, as equally committed to Jesus, the Bible and the Church as we are, reach different conclusions. Sometimes this will puzzle us, but we have to learn that while we are here on earth all things will not become clear, and that it is arrogant to think they will. That is why we need to respect the opinions of others and listen carefully to what they have to say. They may even cause us to think differently. But if on some issues we find ourselves saying with great emphasis 'I believe this to be right, or that to be wrong, and I believe it because I am trying to be loyal to Jesus Christ', then we must have the courage of our convictions and hold firmly to them—at least until fresh insights make us change our minds.

1. QUESTIONS ABOUT SEX AND MARRIAGE

Marriages at risk

It has been said that marriage was never more popular and never more risky than it is today. The risks are obvious. In the circle of most people's friends and neighbours there are some whose marriages are stable, some who are separated or divorced, some who are single parents, some who have re-married, and some who are living together, not yet married and not necessarily intending to be. Marriage continues in popularity but its pattern is changing. Families are smaller. Couples who stay together can expect to remain together, happily or unhappily, for a much longer time than was once possible. They may have another thirty years or more after the children have left home. Partners generally expect a much higher standard of living than was once possible for most people. Many wives go out to work. Many husbands are forced by unemployment to spend hours at home in unwelcome idleness. The wife may be as well (or better) educated than her husband. She is no longer content with a passive role either in their sexual relationship or in the management of the home. She is less likely to be financially dependent and even may be a more important breadwinner than her husband. These changes bring to marriage new opportunities for enrichment and new possibilities for tension and break-up. Some men try to fight against their changing role in the relationship. Some women find it convenient to pretend that it has not happened.

The generation gap subjects the family to further strains. As children go through adolescence, adopting the particular fashions in dress, music, manners and lifestyle in vogue at the time, parents and children often find themselves at odds with one another. This can bring great frustration to grown-ups as they try to keep in communication with their offspring, and despair to the children as they attempt to experience what growing up is all about. Sometimes there are problems at the other end of the age range. There are now nearly four times as many people of pensionable age as there were at the beginning of the century. There are ten times as many over the age of eighty-five. This can put a considerable strain on the younger members of the family. It is sometimes said that they do not look after their elders as once they did, but this is not borne out by facts. There is no increase in the percentage of those who have to live in institutions for the old. The vast majority continue to live in the community and to take an active part in it. If they live in sheltered accommodation or in old people's bungalows, there are usually members of the family nearby who can keep a watchful eye on them. Yet when old people live in with younger members of their family there can be considerable stress on all sides. Some young couples make considerable sacrifices to look after an elderly parent. This is not always to the benefit of the family as a whole.

There are other things which threaten marriage

today. Poverty, still a major factor in Britain, can strain a marriage to breaking point. Rumours of cuts in social security benefits and threats to the health service increase anxiety. There is a painful link between rising unemployment and domestic violence. Boredom and a sense of rejection can lead to alcoholism and crime—both notable marriage breakers. Many of these people with marriages at risk are the victims of the kind of society in which they live. Marriage is a risky business in twentieth century Britain. Little wonder that so many end in divorce.

Sex before marriage

Much of the blame for the present marriage situation is put at the doors of the sexual irresponsibility of the young and recent legislation which makes divorce too easy. Both these criticisms should be taken seriously by Christian people.

There is an old saying that chastity before marriage creates fidelity within marriage. Perhaps it is not so simple as that, yet it is hard not to see some link between sexual freedom which so many young people take for granted and the breakdown of many marriages. The temptation to explore sexual relationships at an early age is no new phenomenon. It is made less resistable today by the ease with which young people can get together without supervision, and the ready availability of contraception. One boy in four and one girl in eight claim to have had sexual intercourse before their eighteenth birthday. Many have sex without taking adequate precautions, or using them carelessly. Thousands of teenage girls have abortions each year, and thousands more have babies. In London one birth in three is illegitimate, and the figure is rising. It is reckoned that one girl in three under twenty years of age is pregnant at the time of marriage, and it has to be questioned whether many of these couples would have decided to get married if they had been more cautious. For the adolescent sex is exciting, puzzling, frightening and full of risk. Where can they find help at a time when there is so much to discover and so much to learn?

Our western sophisticated society is less efficient at helping young people to cope with their growing sexuality than are many more primitive peoples. Modern sex education frequently seems to be confined to advice on 'how to enjoy it' and 'how to avoid getting pregnant'. Little help is available towards an understanding of the deeper significance of their sexual feelings and experiences, or what this has to do with love and marriage.

It is unlikely that sexual morality can ever again be based on hard and fast rules and prohibitions. Young people want to be given the reasons why adults say that some things are right and some are wrong. It is the Christian claim that sex is not given to us by God to be used either for trivial 'kicks' or as a part of a smash and grab power game played by men and women. Sex is for loving. And sexual love is for creation in two ways: the creation and upbringing of children, and the creation of a life-long union between husband and wife. Only in this understanding of the purpose of God in the gift of sex does it become possible to evaluate the rights and wrongs of sexual behaviour. Christianity has a message of good news about love to each succeeding generation. But within that love true freedom can only come through self-discipline. Without that discipline sexual relationships quickly become sordid and frustrating. Many

4

young people experimenting in sexual relationships and only finding disappointment are searching for good news about themselves which the Christian faith can supply. It is our responsibility not to let them down.

'Living together'

Whatever may be the rights and wrongs of pre-marital sex, most people are ready to make a distinction between casual 'sleeping together' (which they probably condemn) and the growing practice of young couples living together for a longer or shorter time before getting married. It is said that over a million couples in Britain are now doing this, and most have no guilty conscience about it. They see it as a healthy and sensible preparation for adult life and (probably) eventual marriage. They deny that this is simply a way of getting 'easy sex', or that they do it because two can live as cheaply as one. They claim that, although not ready for marriage, they have reached a stage in life when they need the emotional and spiritual fulfilment which comes from close companionship. Marriage will come when examinations are finished, a steady job acquired, or the time has come to start a family. Some of the young people who argue in this way are convinced Christians and see no contradiction between their faith and their style of life. Even those who 'live together' but refuse to enter into the formal commitment of marriage because of their own unhappy relationships in the past, or because of disillusionment in seeing the mess so many older people have made of their marriages, nevertheless live in a loving and stable commitment in a way which puts many so-called 'proper marriages' to shame.

How should Christian people evaluate these relationships? Some are convinced that the present situation compels us to rethink our traditional values. Should we not put more emphasis on the inner quality of a relationship and less on the formal and legal trappings which surround it? There are good arguments for this more liberal and less legalistic point of view. But others insist that the traditional teaching of the Church about chastity before marriage points to an ideal which should still be vigorously upheld. They see 'living together' as a modern fashion which can only weaken the moral fabric of society. They argue that sexual intercourse, which is intended by God to express and deepen the commitment of a man and a women to one another cannot be given its full meaning until the obligation of marriage has been solemnly and publicly undertaken. As Dr Jack Dominion has said, 'It is only continuous, reliable and trustworthy relationships which allow for a full enjoyment of the sexual potential, and those are other words for marriage.'

It is the task of the Christian Church to point to the ideal, convinced that what is the will of God must lead to greater good and happiness for all. But Christians also know that many fail to reach that ideal, and they are glad to be entrusted with a Gospel which proclaims the loving kindness of a God who is always more ready to forgive than to condemn.

Divorce

On 1 January 1971, the Divorce Reform Act became law. For the first time in England irretrievable breakdown became the major ground for divorce. The results were far-reaching. The number of divorces soared dramatically. Yet even before the new law came into force, public opinion polls suggested that most people preferred the concept of irretrievable breakdown to the old system when an accusing finger had to be pointed to one of the spouses as a 'guilty party'. It is better to declare a moribund marriage dead than to try to apportion blame. But how could it be proved in a court of law that a marriage had irretrievably broken down? Adultery committed by one partner would be a likely sign that the marriage would be intolerable if it were continued. The behaviour of one, or both, of the parties might make it unreasonable to expect that the relationship should continue. But the new factor was the assumption that if both parties had lived apart continuously for two years and both wished to have the marriage dissolved, it could sensibly be deemed as having already broken down. And even if one of the partners refused to agree to a divorce, the marriage could be dissolved on the application of one of the parties if they had lived continuously apart for five years. Some people felt that this latter provision was harsh on anyone who in principle objected to divorce. But what the court was saying on these occasions was that after five years' separation the evidence would point clearly to the fact that the marriage had in practice ceased to exist, and was therefore no longer qualified to receive legal recognition.

In 1984 a new Act came into force allowing divorce proceedings to begin one year after marriage. This encouragement to couples to consider breaking up their marriage so soon after the wedding was vigorously opposed by most of the Christian Churches.

The Mothers' Union felt that the proposal made it too easy for those who 'want out' when they are still enduring the 'getting to know you' process. The secretary of the Church of England's Board of Social Responsibility regretted that the Government had chosen to introduce this new legislation.

> 'All they have done is to give the impression that if people find things difficult in the early months, as often happens, they are encouraged along the road to divorce.'

Another comment on this new proposal came from Canon G. B. Bentley of Windsor who made an interesting and provocative suggestion.

> 'A marriage which comes to grief during the first "honeymoon" year may be said to have crashed on the runway and failed to get off the ground and it seems reasonable to infer from the disaster that it must have been gravely defective *ab initio*. It could have been that the parties' knowledge of each other had been so defective that in effect they committed themselves to figments of their imagination and not to actual persons. Or they may have entertained a false image of marriage and co-habitation and found themselves unable to cope with the reality. Or again it could be that one or other of them was quite simply unfit for marriage. Whatever the cause, no real or active marriage had been achieved. In my opinion there is much to be said for treating the first year of marriage as integral to its making.'

So the canon argued that failure during the first year should be made a ground for declaring the marriage null and void. It has never really existed, therefore there can be no reason for divorce.

This created a lively debate with most people

recognizing Canon Bentley's wish to be compassionate. But his view was widely challenged. If marriage does not begin with the taking of mutual vows, when does it start? Vows are vows, and should be taken with absolute seriousness on the wedding day itself. If couples feel they must have a 'try-out' before marriage, this should happen before and not after taking solemn vows to one another.

It is generally accepted that the high rate of divorce today represents a tragic failure in our life as a nation, and that a fair proportion of those broken marriages could have been saved if there had been the will to do so. In Britain there are now about one hundred and forty thousand divorces a year. This not only brings unhappiness to the couples concerned and to their immediate circle of family and friends but as many as one hundred and sixty thousand children are involved each year. All this represents a huge cost to parents and children in feelings of guilt, rejection, depression and anxiety. There is also a big price to be paid by the nation in terms of legal aid, child care and social security benefits. The victims of broken marriages need understanding and practical support not only from those professionally involved in the legal, medical and social welfare services, but also from friends and neighbours. The Christian Churches, with their commitment to loving care and compassion have a special responsibility here.

Christians should be sympathetic to divorcees. But what should be their attitude to divorce itself? All agree that marriage is intended by God to be a life-long partnership. Disagreement comes in attempting to answer two further questions: *Can* a marriage be dissolved? Are there circumstances when a marriage *should* be dissolved? One view is that when Jesus said

'What God has joined together, man must not separate', he was declaring the intrinsic indissolubility of marriage. By the nature of things, men and women become one flesh which nothing can undo. This is the view held by the Roman Catholic Church, though their practice of declaring some marriages null after due investigation seems to many people to be an alternative method of divorce under another name. A view held by many Christians is that the New Testament is less clear on the matter than those who take the hard-line claim. Mark quotes Jesus as teaching that although God intended that men and women should enter into a permanent relationship, the Jewish law allowed divorce as a concession to human weakness.[1] Did Jesus present indissolubility as an ideal to be aimed at whilst acknowledging that because 'men's minds are closed' or because 'you are so hard to teach' many will fall short of perfection? Our attempt to discover what Jesus actually taught is made more difficult by Matthew's account in which Jesus is reported as saying that a man may not divorce his wife 'for any cause other than unchastity'.[2] Does this reflect the practice which had developed in the early church at the time Matthew was writing? Were they finding the teaching of Jesus too absolute, and were already allowing divorce on certain grounds in accordance with the Jewish teaching in which many of them had grown up? Paul certainly suggested that a divorce was permissible in situations when one partner had adopted Christianity and the other had remained a pagan.[3]

Today the practice of most of the Churches is to recognize the necessity of divorce under certain circumstances whilst acknowledging the ideal of a lifelong partnership as the undoubted will of God. Dr

10

Stephen Orchard of the British Council of Churches speaking to students in London University said:

'I think it is much more likely that Jesus accepted divorce as a regrettable accommodation to human frailty, and that his words "let no man put asunder" were addressed to families and communities who disapproved of a particular marriage, and set out to part husband and wife, or possibly a warning against adultery. In other words, whatever that text says to the divorce courts is nothing to what it says to a South African government deliberately isolating husbands from their families, or a Soviet regime which puts dissenters many days journey away from those who love them.'

Remarriage after divorce

A high proportion of those who have been divorced decide to marry again. Some second marriages fail, and the number of second failures is increasing. But many are happy and successful. Most of those who enter a second marriage after divorce are content to have a civil ceremony in the registrar's office. But some want a church wedding. Whilst some do this for show, or at the insistence of parents, others feel that because the first marriage was a failure there is all the more reason why the second should be celebrated with solemn vows and appropriate prayers. Few problems in recent years have given the Churches more anxiety than what their attitude should be to those who ask the church to celebrate a second marriage with a partner still living. What conditions, if any, should be laid down? This is a particular problem for the Church of England. As the established Church of the land it is responsible for most church weddings. Parishioners have a historic right to be married in their own parish church even if they never attend it on other occasions. In both national and diocesan synods this has been a matter of long and serious debate. There have been hours of talk and hundreds of pages of print. But no clear policy has emerged.

Whatever rights parishioners may have, in English law the parish priest has the right to refuse to conduct a 'second marriage' if his conscience will not allow it. The Church Union (the 'high church' pressure group) has campaigned throughout the debate on behalf of those who take the absolute view.

> 'We trust that no bishop will authorise and no priest solemnise a "second marriage" except in the rare case where it can be established beyond reasonable doubt that the previous union was not a true and binding marriage.'

A proposal favoured by some is to make a clear distinction between secular and religious views of marriage. Let everyone be married in the registrar's office according to the legal requirements of marriage as a civil contract. Let those who believe marriage to be a sacrament in which the grace of God is sought to enable them to fulfil life-long vows come to church and make their solemn commitment within an act of Christian worship. Under this system the Church would be free to impose its own marriage discipline appropriate to those who sincerely claim to be members of the Body of Christ. But there are those who object to this proposal because they see it as the Church opting out of its wider responsibilities to the nation. Marriages still provide the clergy with a valuable point of contact with a large section of the public at a very impressionable moment in their lives. Some take very seriously their responsibility to prepare young couples for Christian marriage. Many more should. But how to find the right compromise between pastoral concern and New Testament values is a question which will continue to occupy the mind of the Churches in this country for a long time to come.

The Church of England's two Convocations (York in 1938 and Canterbury in 1957) expressly forbade church weddings for anyone with a partner still living. But this prohibition did not have the force of law and with the rapid increase of divorce some clergy began to exercise their legal right to conduct 'second marriages' when they thought fit. Sometimes they asked the approval of the bishop or sought his advice, some acted quite independently. Some bishops approved. Some strongly disapproved. Some encouraged a service of blessing after a civil wedding. Others saw it as the thin end of the wedge. Eventually a scheme was worked out which would allow the remarriage of divorced persons under certain circumstances. It would be the responsibility of the parish priest to interview the couple and to inquire into the circumstances of the previous breakdown. What was the degree of guilt? Was there a desire to repent? What were the likely prospects of success in the new marriage? A detailed report of this inquiry with recommendations would be sent to the bishop by the parish priest. The bishop would submit it to an expert advisory panel before making his final decision whether the church wedding could go ahead.

These ideas were tossed backwards and forwards between the bishops, the General Synod, the dioceses and the parishes. No clear line of action emerged. Finally it was passed back to the bishops for a ruling, and they resolved to leave it to the local clergy to decide. It was a return to square one. Those who hoped for a clear ruling were disappointed. Others felt it was the only honest decision in the light of many conflicting opinions in the Church. It is now thought that about a third of the Church of England clergy will normally refuse a second marriage, about a third will pick and choose according to circumstances, and the rest are likely to marry more or less anyone. A divorcee in England wishing to marry again in his parish church will have to take pot luck according to the sort of vicar who rules over the parish where he or his bride lives.

After so much discussion it is unlikely that this matter will be raised again officially for some time. The *Church Times* was probably correct when it expressed the belief that the only practical decision had been reached 'given the nature of the Church of England and the fact of its link with the State'. It admitted that the bishops would 'no doubt be criticized in the world at large as an example of the Church at its wooliest' but concluded that 'the solution to the impasse, though far from perfect, is the only solution likely to stand any chance of success. If disorder appears to result, it will at least be licensed disorder.'

Homosexual relationships

Until recently homosexuality was seldom discussed openly in conversation and only hinted at in books and plays. Now the subject receives much publicity, not least from homosexuals themselves. The 'Gay Rights' movement is a powerful lobby. Until 1967 homosexual acts between two males were illegal and could incur severe penalties. Since the passing of the Sexual Offences Act in that year this ceased to be illegal provided that the parties were over the age of twenty-one, and that what was done was in private and with mutual consent. The Act applied only in England and Wales, and members of the armed forces and the crews of merchant ships were excluded.

Public opinion has tended to remain hostile to homosexuals in spite of the change in the law. They are subjected to constant snide jokes by comedians and are caricatured in plays, TV programmes and novels. Many ordinary folk look upon them with suspicion as being 'different'. Attempts in some reports from the Churches to change public attitudes have not been notably successful. Why should this continue to be so?

There is strong biblical evidence to suggest that homosexual activity is against the will of God because it is 'against nature'. Paul wrote of those men who 'lust after one another, males behaving indecently with males' as breaking all the rules of conduct. 'They know well enough the just decree of God, that those who behave like this deserve to die, and yet they do it.'[4] Many Christian people today echo Paul's severe condemnation, and insist that the Church must hold firmly to his teaching. But others want to question whether the apostle's view that homosexuality is 'against nature' can be maintained today in the light of contemporary medical and psychological knowledge. It is reckoned that there are about a million homosexuals in England. It is now known (as Paul could not know) that the true homosexual can no more change his sexual orientation than a 'normal' person can stop being heterosexual. It is a 'given' condition, even though medical experts are uncertain how it comes about. It is unjust to tell a homosexual to 'repent' as some do. Yet Christian opinion generally insists that although the homosexual cannot be blamed for his sexual orientation, he commits sin if he attempts to indulge in sexual activity with another male. This is seen as the moral equivalent of fornication in a heterosexual. But there is a minority Christian opinion which believes that there *may* be circumstances in which homosexuals should be able to claim the same moral right to express their love for one another in physical ways within a stable relationship as is allowed to men and women in marriage.

This was the conclusion reached very tentatively by a group set up in 1974 by the Church of England Board for Social Responsibility to examine the biblical, theological, medical and legal aspects of the subject. In its most discussed section the report, published in 1979, stated:

> 'In the light of some evidence we have received we do not think it possible to deny that there are circumstances in which individuals may justifiably choose to enter into a homosexual relationship with the hope of enjoying a companionship and physical expression of sexual love similar to that found in marriage. . . . Such a relationship could not be regarded as a moral or social equivalent of marriage; it would be bound to have a private and experimental character which marriage cannot and should not have. Nevertheless fidelity and permanence although not institutionally required would undoubtedly do much to sustain and enhance its genuinely personal commitment and aspiration.'[5]

The report was not generally welcomed. Many Christians thought it went too far. Many homosexuals thought it did not go far enough. In a speech to the Church of England General Synod the Archbishop of Canterbury hoped that the report would be used to 'promote the kind of informed discussion which would combat the silly insinuations and innuendos, the casual contempt and unthinking mockery of homosexuality which so often pass for discussion even in Church circles'. He himself preferred to see homosexuality neither as a sin nor sickness but as a handicap, a state in which the fulfilment of heterosexual love and marriage is denied.

> 'The best way forward now, I suggest, is for the Church to combat with vigour the hatred and denigration of the homosexual which is widespread in our society and to try to come to a balanced understanding of their difficulties and their potential . . . always bearing in mind the new ways in which we have come to view those who are handicapped, and to learn from them.'

The report *Homosexual Relationships* was published, discussed and then dropped by the Church as a hot potato. It is a subject that most people prefer not to talk about. The brash and often militant stance of the Gay Rights movement serves only to prevent many people from taking them and their cause with the seriousness they deserve. But both the report itself and the Archbishop of Canterbury's comments should encourage responsible Christian people to show concern for this considerable number of their fellow human beings and to think about the contribution that the Christian faith could bring to a solution of the dilemma which so many of them have to face. The report itself makes a strong plea for compassionate understanding.

'Homosexuals, through no fault of their own, find

themselves in a situation of great difficulty in which many of the moral guidelines normally available do not apply and in which there is little general sympathy or understanding. They need the assurance that solutions adopted by them in good faith—and we are talking here of mature adults capable of responsible choice—will not be condemned out of hand by people who cannot know all the circumstances in each case.'

QUESTIONS FOR DISCUSSION

1. What do you think are the particular problems which face a young couple getting married today? Do you agree that special difficulties can be caused by the generation gap and by the claims of elderly relatives? Are there ways in which the local churches can provide some help to meet these difficulties?

2. In view of the high rate of marriage failure today, should there be more provision for marriage education for those about to be married and more support for those already married who are facing difficulties? How can this be done?

3. What are the advantages and disadvantages of couples living together before marriage? What view do you take of the suggestion made by Canon Bentley on page 8?

4. What support can or should the local church give to single parent families and those who have been divorced?

5. Under what circumstances (if any) should a divorcee with a partner still living be permitted to have a second marriage in church?

6. The Archbishop of Canterbury has urged that 'the best way forward is for the Church to combat with vigour the hatred and denigration of the homosexual which is widespread in our society, and to try to come to a balanced understanding of their difficulties and potential.' What practical steps could be taken to do this in your local community and church?

Groups discussing these questions will be greatly helped by inviting a local marriage guidance counsellor, social worker, school counsellor or solicitor to join them. In any discussion on question 6, you will find it useful if it is possible to ask a Christian who is a homosexual to talk to you about the problems he faces in the light of his faith and his sexual orientation.

Notes
1. Mark 10. 1–12
2. Matthew 5. 31–32
3. 1 Corinthians 7. 12–19
4. Romans. 1 26–32
5. *Homosexual Relationships,* paragraph 168.

For Further Reading
The Future of the Family, Wendy Green (Mowbray)
The Family and Marriage in Britain, Ronald Fletcher (Pelican)

Ask the Family, Jeanette Longfield, Bedford Square Press (NCVO)

I give you this ring, Edward Patey (Mowbray)

Marriage in the Local Church (British Council of Churches)

Homosexual Relationships (CIO Publishing)

Christian Attitudes to Homosexuality, Peter Coleman (SCM)

2. QUESTIONS ABOUT LIFE AND DEATH

Professor T. F. Torrance, the Church of Scotland theologian, read through the pages of the Warnock Report on Human Fertilisation with increasing pessimism and horror.

'Medical Science has brought us to an ultimate boundary beyond which a God-fearing society committed to the sanctity of marriage and the structure of the human family may not go.'[1]

In this chapter we will discuss some of these dangerous boundaries in matters of life and death which are giving many other people besides the professor cause for concern.

The Gillick Judgement

It is illegal for a man to have sexual relations with a girl under the age of sixteen. But this is not an infrequent occurrence, and many under-age girls find it prudent to go to their doctors or a clinic for contraceptive advice. This has put the medical profession in a difficult position and is a matter of urgent anxiety for parents of girls in their early teens. Clear guidance is needed on the medical, legal and moral position. In 1974 the Department of Health and Social Security issued a memorandum advising doctors that the provision of contraceptives to girls under sixteen did not incur criminal liability or infringe parental rights if they took care to act with professional responsibility. They should do all in their power to persuade the child to confide in her parents or allow them to do so, and this should be the normal practice. But if the principle of confidentiality between doctors and patients were to be abandoned for children under sixteen, this might cause some of them not to seek any professional advice. Particularly in the case of young people whose parents were unconcerned, unresponsive or grossly disturbed, it would be right to give contraceptive advice and treatment without parental knowledge or consent.

Mrs Victoria Gillick, a Cambridgeshire housewife, was determined that none of her five daughters should be able to get birth control advice whilst they were still under sixteen without her knowledge and consent. She wrote to her area health authority formally forbidding any of their staff to do so. She was equally determined that this should be the rule in all other families as well. The acting administrator replied that the health authority held the view that 'the treatment prescribed by a doctor was a matter for the doctor's clinical judgement taking into account all the facts of the case'. In response she conducted a skilful publicity campaign, went to law, and obtained a High Court ruling which declared the memorandum issued by the Department of Health and Social Security in 1974 to be unlawful. The court ruled that 'no doctor or other professional person employed by the area health authority might give contraceptive or abortion advice or treatment to any child below the age of sixteen without the prior knowledge and consent of the child's parent or guardian.' Mrs Gillick declared her victory to be a shot in the arm for all those parents who thought what was happening was wrong. The Chief Rabbi greeted the High Court ruling in favour of Mrs Gillick as being 'of immense relief to all who seek to reassert the rights and duties of parents and who see a major cause for the rampant rise of crime and vice in the widespread breakdown of family life'. But there were many others who maintained that whatever might be appropriate for Mrs Gillick's daughters in their closely-knit Roman Catholic family could not be applied in many other instances where families were not united and where parents and children had very little sympathy or understanding of one another.

A spokesman for the British Medical Association said:

> 'People feel outraged that someone could give their fourteen-year-old daughter the pill without their knowledge. But the trouble is that the young girls who need this help do not come from secure middle class families. If parents must be told about all medical treatment the girls would stop coming to see their doctors. But this would not stop them having sex.'

The Central President of the Mothers' Union and the chairperson of its Social Concerns Committee wrote to the *Church Times:*

> 'Prolonged and prayerful debate has led us to accept that the prescription of contraceptives for girls under sixteen (with or without parental knowledge or consent) may in some circumstances be the lesser evil when the alternative is abortion or the birth of an unwanted or unloved child. We also recognize that there are situations in which the needs and desires of parents are in

direct conflict with those of their child. In these circumstances we have chosen to support the child as the more vulnerable person. The Mothers' Union is, and always has been, anxious to explore every possible way of encouraging teenagers to practise abstinence. However we recognize that the DHSS must provide for all families, and not only for the great majority of parents (whether Christian or not) who care. This is where we differ from Mrs Gillick even while recognizing her commitment and her sincerity.'

In giving judgement in the High Court in favour of Mrs Gillick, Lord Justice Parker admitted that the court was concerned only with the legal position. He recognized that 'respectable and responsible people might hold different strong and sincere views as to the moral, religious and ethical questions arising out of the case'. It was clear that there would be another chapter in the saga of the Gillick judgement. The Department of Health and Social Security was given leave to appeal to the House of Lords. The case was heard before five Law Lords, and their judgement was published on 17 October 1985. By the slender majority of 3 votes to 2, the High Court judgement was overturned, the appeal from the Department of Health and Social Security upheld, and Mrs Gillick's plea rejected. The statements made by the five judges, including those of the two who dissented, are of great interest and importance, and will be discussed for many years to come.

Lord Fraser, who presided, said that after careful consideration of the relevant statutes, he had come to the conclusion that there was no provision which compelled him to hold that a girl under sixteen lacked the legal capacity to consent to contraceptive advice, examination or treatment provided that she had sufficient understanding and intelligence to know what was involved. The major questions for consideration was the right of the parent in these matters. Mrs Gillick sought the absolute right to be informed and to veto such advice and treatment even in the most unusual circumstances which might arise. Lord Fraser pointed out that parental right to control the child existed not for the benefit of the parent but of the child.

> 'It is contrary to the ordinary experience of mankind, at least in Western Europe in the present century, to say that a child remained in fact under the complete control of his parents until he attained the definite age of majority, and that on attaining that age, he suddenly acquired independence. In practice, most wise parents relax their control gradually as the child develops, and encourage him to become increasingly independent. ... It would be unrealistic for the courts not to recognize these facts. Social customs change, and the law ought to, and does in fact, have regard to such changes when they are of such major importance.'

Lord Fraser believed that in the overwhelming majority of cases the best judges of a child's welfare were the parents, but there might be circumstances when the doctor was the better judge of the medical advice and treatment most conducive to the girl's well-being.

> 'It is notorious that children of both sexes are often reluctant to confide in their parents about sexual matters ... and to abandon the principle of confidentiality for contraceptive advice to girls under sixteen might cause some not to seek pro-

fessional advice at all, thus exposing them to the immediate risk of pregnancy and sexually transmitted disease.'

For this reason he believed that the doctor must be entitled in some cases to give contraceptive advice and treatment to girls under sixteen without the consent or even knowledge of her parents, provided that he was satisfied:

1. That the girl would, although under sixteen, understand his advice.
2. That he could not persuade her to inform her parents, or to allow him to inform them, that she was seeking contraceptive advice.
3. That she was very likely to have sexual intercourse with or without contraceptive treatment.
4. That unless she received contraceptive treatment her physical or mental health, or both, were likely to suffer.
5. That her best interests required him to give her contraceptive advice or treatment, or both, without parental consent.

These five provisos may prove to be a very important safeguard for the medical profession in this difficult area of decision making.

Lord Scarman, who concurred with the majority verdict, also believed that the law had to take into account changing social circumstances. He saw three new relevant facts which the law would neglect at its peril:

contraception as a subject for medical advice and treatment;

the increasing independence of young people;

the changed status of women.

He added:

'If the law should impose upon the process of

growing up fixed limits where nature keeps only a continuous process, the price would be artificiality and lack of realism in an area where the law must be sensitive to human development and social change.'

Two of the judges dissented from the majority decision. Lord Brandon argued that because it was unlawful for a man to have sexual intercourse with a girl under sixteen, it follows

'that for any person to promote, encourage or facilitate the commission of such an act might itself be a criminal offence and must, in any event, be contrary to public policy.'

This applied equally to parent, doctor or social worker. He also rejected the argument that a girl was likely to have intercourse anyway, whether or not she obtained contraceptive advice. He believed that the refusal to give such advice was more likely to discourage illicit intercourse for fear of pregnancy.

Lord Templeman gave other reasons why he dissented from the majority verdict. He did not believe that a girl of sixteen was mature enough to understand all the issues involved and was incapable of making a balanced judgement. He was also concerned about the rights of parents. The doctor who provided contraceptive facilities without the parents' knowledge deprived them of the opportunity to protect the girl from sexual intercourse by persuading her and helping her, or by the exercise of parental power. He thought that a parent would sooner or later find out the truth, and might do so in circumstances which brought about a complete rupture of good relations between members of the family, and between the family and the doctor. He also had an objection on moral grounds. The secret provision of contraceptives to a

27

girl under sixteen offended basic principles of morality and religion which 'ought not to be sabotaged by kind permission of the National Health Service'.

As was to be expected, response to the House of Lords' judgement was widespread and various. The Bishop of Birmingham (Dr Montefiore) issued a statement on behalf of the Church of England's Board for Social Responsibility, of which he is the chairman.

> 'The Gillick case has raised many critically important questions about a child's development towards maturity, the role both of parental responsibility and of the medical practitioner. The past years have shown that many views are held with great sincerity on this matter. The narrowness of the vote in the Law Lords' ruling reflects the differences of opinion that exist more generally in society. Now that this ruling has been made, the Board believes that every effort must be made to ensure that medical practitioners observe the conditions rigorously. In this respect, the five guidelines outlined in Lord Fraser's summing up are a significant safeguard. We recognize that these guidelines place new responsibilities on medical practitioners. If they are to be met a considerable amount of time will need to be spent with each individual. We call upon the DHSS to ensure there is a very close monitoring of the way they are implemented.'

The Church of England Children's Society, though very concerned about the damage caused by underage sexuality, was happy that the decision had been taken to make the guidelines clear cut.

> 'In most families parents will know what their children are doing: but it is the minority we work with where relations have almost broken down.

The new ruling will be most helpful in that doctors will have room to make a judgement. A very vulnerable group will at last have somewhere to turn.'

The Mothers' Union, taking the stance it had maintained all along, was 'relieved that doctors are now able to prescribe for girls whose parents don't care, or are not interested'.

On the contrary the so-called pro-life organizations took a very different view. The Society for the Protection of the Unborn Child said that the judgement entirely destroyed any protection from sexual exploitation of young girls under sixteen. The CARE Trust (formerly the Nationwide Festival of Light) pledged itself to press for speedy legislation to 'uphold the rights of parents and ensure the protection of children'.

The position taken by Mrs Gillick had the support of the great majority of Roman Catholics from the beginning. In a statement Cardinal Basil Hume made it clear that the Law Lords' judgement would make no difference to the Roman Catholic position.

'The judgement of the House of Lords while clarifying the present state of the law does not, and cannot, decide what is morally right or wrong. In no way does it alter or affect the moral principles and teaching of the Catholic Church concerning contraception. As is well known, Catholic moral teaching does not permit the use of artificial means of contraception. This applies irrespective of age. Whatever one's legal opinion or one's moral stance, the fact that such issues needed to be raised in this way is a grave reflection on our contemporary society. It is tragic that our young people should be subjected to so many influences which contribute to sexual permissiveness and a lowering of moral standards. The strictness of the Church's teaching, which the bishops will constantly uphold, underlines the importance of promoting stable family life and of developing in parents and children healthy relationships and an atmosphere of mutual trust. On these the future of our children and our society depends.'

In a subsequent statement the Cardinal expressed his regret that such a moral issue should have had to be debated in a court of law. He doubted

'the wisdom of choosing the courts as a place to wage this entirely justifiable campaign. Legal action immediately and inevitably raised other complex and disputed questions; the major ones were about the legal limits of parental responsibility, how to protect children of irresponsible or problem parents and how to defend medical confidentiality. My fear is that after the Lords' ruling there will be some who of set purpose will seek to extend the discretion now allowed them by the law. There will be some vulnerable young people who will now believe that sexual activity outside marriage is condoned, even if not positively approved, by the law.'

The highest court of law in the land has made its judgement. This will have disappointed many. Many others (perhaps the majority) will believe that the best practical decision has been reached on this difficult issue. It is important to study each side of the argument carefully. As in all the great questions for today those who are 'for' and those who are 'against' have much to learn from one another. The debate continues.

Infertility and the Warnock Report

Until recently little attention was given to the plight of those, perhaps one in every ten, who find that they are unable to have a child. Some accept the situation as inevitable and find other outlets for their creative instincts. Some are able to have a child by adoption, though this solution is less readily available than it once was. In particular there are very few babies suitable for adoption by a young couple as their first child. Some even see a moral value in their involuntary infertility and believe that because of the overpopulation of the world it would be wrong for them to seek a cure for their situation as if childlessness were a disease. Yet most couples marry with the expectation of having children and are deeply disappointed when it becomes clear that it is not possible for them. Friends and relatives drop hints 'that it is time you started a family'. The couple themselves may feel a deep sense of failure. 'If other people can have babies, why not us?' When medical tests prove negative, the impact can be shattering. If the husband is found to be the infertile partner, he may develop a great sense of guilt that he is unable to give his wife the child they both want so much. It is for couples like this that medical science can give the help they so badly need. It is for them that new techniques in the treatment of infertility such as artificial insemination and *in vitro* fertilization may come as such a Godsend. It is as recently as 1978 that the first 'test-tube baby' was born. Since then progress has been rapid. Yet there is a growing concern that the medical profession, intoxicated by the success of their experiments, may be tempted to push ahead too fast.

In response to this public disquiet the Government

set up a Commission of Inquiry in 1982 under the distinguished chairmanship of Dame Mary Warnock. Its task was 'to examine the social, ethical and legal implications of recent and potential developments in the field of assisted human reproduction'. The report, published in 1984, was widely discussed, and had a mixed reception. The Church of England Board for Social Responsibility welcomed the report's acknowledgement that 'the issues raised reflect fundamental moral and often religious questions which have taxed philosophers and others all down the ages'. The pro-life organizations such as Care and the Society for the Protection of the Unborn Child launched a vigorous attack on many of its proposals. The Roman Catholic Church found little with which to agree in it. Professor Torrance, already quoted above, found it outraged his conscience at a deeper level than almost anything else he had read in recent years. But middle of the road opinion in the Church of England and the Methodist Church was ready to see the report in a much more positive and hopeful light, and to agree with many of its major conclusions.

When discussing these new techniques for the treatment of infertility a number of major moral questions have to be faced. Are there limits beyond which humans should not interfere with the course of nature? Do methods such as artificial insemination, 'test-tube' fertilization and surrogate motherhood have a detrimental effect on the institution of marriage? Is the human embryo, even in its earliest days, a person or potential person who must have the maximum protection of the law? These are complex questions with no easy answers. Only the main issues for discussion can be indicated in the following pages.

Artificial insemination, the first technique to be

discussed by Warnock, has already been in successful use for a number of years. Artificial insemination by the husband (AIH) involves placing the husband's semen into his wife's body by means other than by sexual intercourse. It is necessary when for physical or psychological reasons the man is unable to perform the act of intercourse, but is capable of producing semen. Most people find no moral objection to this procedure which simply assists the natural process and enables it to reach its desired fulfilment. Artificial insemination by donor (AID) raises a more difficult question because the semen is provided not by the husband but by an anonymous donor. The procedure is called for when the husband is infertile or there is a danger of a hereditary disease being transmitted by the male. Forty years ago the Archbiship of Canterbury set up a committee which said that 'artificial insemination with donated semen involves a breach of marriage. It violates the exclusive union between husband and wife.' The Roman Catholic Church in its response to Warnock makes the same point:

> 'We think AID is not in the interests of the child, the family, or society, and, accordingly should not be available as a publicly approved or organised service. Children have a right to be born the true child of a married couple.'[2]

The Warnock Committee clearly saw that AID would be increasingly practised and believed that there could be no objection if it were available on a properly organized basis. They did not agree with those who claim that it is an adulterous act. No personal relationship is involved between the mother and the donor, and the identity of the true father of the AID child will normally be unknown to the mother and unascertainable by her. The Board for

Social Responsibility of the Church of England, responding to Warnock took the same view, disagreeing with the Roman Catholic statement. It asserted that:

> 'It is possible for a couple today to have in good conscience the conviction that the semen of a third party imparts nothing alien to the marriage relationship and does not adulterate it as physical union would.'[3]

More positively the Church of England response was able to state that the majority of its members on the Board for Social Responsibility agreed with the Warnock Committee that 'those engaged in AID are in their own view involved in a positive affirmation of the family'. At present the child conceived by AID is deemed illegitimate and registered as 'father unknown'. The Board for Social Responsibility agrees with the Warnock recommendation that such children should be registered as legitimate and at the age of eighteen should have access to information concerning the donor's ethnic origin, and genetic health. The Church of England Board was very positive that it was entirely inappropriate that donors should sell their semen for gain. 'Semen is not a commodity to be bought and sold: it is the God-given means of making possible the gift of new human life.'

When it comes to consider *in vitro* fertilization (IVF) (popularly called 'test-tube' babies) the Warnock report enters a much more complex area. Here the techniques used are so new that moral judgements are difficult to make except by those who want to respond immediately with total condemnation and without further thought. Neither the Warnock Committee nor the Church of England's Board for Social Responsibility were prepared to do that. *In vitro* fertilization is a technique by which the ovum is removed from the woman's body and fertilized by a man's semen in the laboratory. After fertilization the embryo is allowed to develop for a day or so in the 'test-tube' before being returned to the woman's body to continue its growth naturally. This method is used with women who can produce healthy eggs and have a normal uterus, but have damaged or diseased fallopian tubes. This condition applies to no more than five per cent of infertile couples, but for them it offers the only possibility of having a baby of their own.

To many people this seems to be taking us into the world of science fiction. The very phrase 'test-tube baby' has a Frankenstein ring to it. A more serious anxiety is whether this is a further deviation from the God-given method of having children by the love-making of the parents. Is this turning the hospital laboratory into a baby factory? The Warnock committee did not think so. They saw IVF as an acceptable means of treating infertility and recommended that it should continue to be available on the National Health Service. The Church of England Board for Social Responsibility gave this careful consideration. Like the Warnock committee they were anxious that IVF, still in its early stages and very expensive to operate, should not divert much needed funds from other areas of infertility treatment. They were also worried about the effect of this process on marriage and family life. But as only a very few couples will ever be likely to need this treatment or be suitable for it, they were ready to accept the positive recommendations of the Warnock report.

In January 1985 Mrs Kim Cotton had a baby in a Barnet hospital. The event hit the headlines in the national press, caused much discussion on television and gave rise to urgent questions in Parliament. The reason for this unusual attention was because Mrs Cotton had been paid by an American couple to have a baby on their behalf, fertilized by AID with the sperm of the husband. The arrangement was transacted by a commercial agency dealing with these matters. This procedure, known as surrogacy or womb leasing, is being used increasingly in the United States. It is undertaken by couples wishing to have a baby when the woman has severe pelvic disorder or has suffered repeated miscarriages. Although it may provide the only possibility for some couples to have a child genetically related to one of them, the weight of public opinion is strongly against it. It is seen as a further intolerable intrusion by a third party into the intimate relationship of marriage, and as inconsistent with human dignity that a woman should lease her womb for profit. The Council for Science and Society sees surrogate motherhood as exploitative as prostitution, and the Law Society has declared it to be the 'deliberate engineering of an illegitimate child'. The Warnock Committee came to the conclusion:

> 'Even in compelling medical circumstances the danger of exploitation of one human being by another appears to the majority of us to far outweigh the potential benefit in almost every case. That people should treat others as a means to their own ends, however desirable the consequences, must always by liable to moral objections.'[4]

In the light of this, Warnock recommended that the operation of agencies whose purpose was to recruit women for surrogate pregnancy or to arrange for individual couples to use their services should be a criminal offence, and that professionals and others involved in the establishment of a surrogate pregnancy should be criminally liable. The greater part of both Church opinion and that of the general public endorses this recommendation. There is a widespread repugnance to any commercial transaction involving surrogacy. But the Warnock Committee recognized that private arrangements might (and probably would) take place, and two of the committee in a minority statement insisted that the door should be left open wide enough to admit some surrogacy arrangements which might, as a last resort, be beneficial to the couple concerned provided that there would be 'no place for commercial operators in surrogacy just as there is no place for commercial adoption agencies'. A committee set up by the Free Church Federal Council to examine the problems of childlessness also suggested that the bearing of a child for another *could* be seen not as an undertaking that trivializes childbearing (as commercial pregnancy does) but as a deliberate and thoughtful act of generosity on the part of one woman to another. But many will prefer to agree with the Roman Catholic Church which opposes surrogacy in any shape or form as a violation of human dignity.

'The proper context of human procreation is that exclusive sexual union which is called marriage in which human affection and exclusive and open-ended commitment, and the transmission of the bodily life of the partners, form the context in which the child is helped to find and form its own identity. *Deliberate* rupturing of that context does indeed treat human bodily life and capacities immorally.'[5]

37

These various points of view demonstrate how difficult it is to make clear-cut moral judgements on intensely personal situations.

There is not space in this book to discuss the many other important and fascinating issues raised in the Warnock Report. Those who wish to study the matter further should read the report itself (it is very well written) and some of the responses which have been made to it. But one further problem must be mentioned because it is the most controversial of all. When embryos are fertilized in the laboratory for an IVF procedure, there are usually some 'spares' which will not be replaced in the woman. Doctors are convinced that research on these spare embryos may be able to increase their knowledge of the early stages of human development. This may enable significant advances in the treatment of infertility, and of such congenital disease as cystic fibrosis, muscular dystrophy, Downs Syndrome (mongolism) and haemophilia. This would clearly be most desirable. The moral argument centres round the question: is an embryo of a few days old a human being or only a potential human being? If from the moment of conception it is a person, then to experiment on it would be to use a person as a laboratory object. One newspaper correspondent, supporting this view, wrote:

> 'In consigning the weakest and smallest of our fellow humans to be bred in laboratories and to live and die in the aid of experimental results, we would degrade ourselves and our every claim to respect the rights of man.'

The Rt Revd Maurice Wood, formerly Bishop of Norwich, is even more emphatic:

> 'Not only is the Christian conscience of the nation being more widely aroused in compas-

sionate concern for the life of defenceless human embryos, but men and women of the broadest ethical and moral principle are beginning to realise that to open this Pandora's Box of genetic engineering is to endanger the very basis of human and family life as we know it.'

But is the argument as clear cut as that? A Harley Street doctor has pointed out that seventy per cent of all human embryos are lost during pregnancy. If the embryo of a few days old is really a 'defenceless human being', why he asks, does God allow such a high proportion of 'human beings' to die before birth? The Archbishop of York, Dr John Habgood, sees the human embryo as 'a bundle of potentialities which are, and will remain, mere potentialities unless a great deal more happens to them of which the first step is implantation. It is, in my view, absurd to talk about a fertilised ovum as if it were in some sense already a human person.'

When does the human embryo become a 'person'? This is the wrong question. The development of the human personality is a gradual process, beginning with conception and reaching its fulfilment in the life-long pattern of an ever-widening circle of relationships with other human persons, and with God. From the start the embryo must be afforded some protection (as Warnock recommends) but that protection need not be absolute until individual development is about to begin. Warnock accepts the scientific evidence that this certainly does not occur within the first fourteen days after conception, and so recommends that under a licence laying down clear conditions spare embryos 'resulting from IVF procedures may be used for research in particular medical areas'. After fourteen days all research should be illegal. It is also recommended that embryos should not be created specifically for research purposes. These recommendations were supported by a majority of the members of the Church of England Board for Social Responsibility, though it is probable that the wider membership of the Church would prefer Parliament to pass a law making all research illegal. The response of the Roman Catholic Church to the Warnock Report on this issue was absolutely clear that 'no research on any human embryo should be permitted except for the benefit of that particular embryo'. It is evident that Christians are deeply divided on this subject.

Are scientists playing at being God? Perhaps so. But it may be that God himself has placed these new powers into our hands for a purpose. If embryo research could lead to a relief of the 75,000 women in Britain who have miscarriages each year, and the 14,000 Britons who annually are born seriously handicapped with congenital defects in body or mind, it may be that the God whose powers the scientists are assuming is the One who is full of compassion and great mercy. The research which is so much feared may prove to be not the work of the devil but the gift of a loving God.

Abortion

Few moral issues raise so much emotion and such strongly held (and opposing) viewpoints as the question of abortion. Dr John Stott, the respected evangelical leader, once said:

> 'How can we speak of the "termination of pregnancy" when what we really mean is the destruction of human life? How can we talk of

therapeutic abortion when pregnancy is not a disease and when abortion is not a cure but a killing?'

But there are many Christian leaders and church commissions who do not see the question in such clear terms. Those who take the conservative view believe that the foetus is a living person and must be safeguarded at all costs right from the moment of conception. That cost may include danger to the health (or even life) of the mother, and the risk that the child may be severely handicapped from birth. The radical position believes that it is entirely within the rights of the mother to decide whether or not she will bear the child which she has conceived. Between these two extremes lies a whole spectrum of opinion.

Society must lay down some general principles about the termination of pregnancy and embody these principles in law. This is necessary not only to safeguard the rights of the mother and the unborn child, but also to protect the integrity of the medical profession, and the confidence of the public in it. But laws of this nature are notoriously difficult to draft, and even more difficult to enforce.

The present law (which does not extend to Northern Ireland) is the Abortion Act of 1967. This permitted an abortion to be carried out if two medical practitioners were of the opinion formed in good faith:

(i) that the continuance of the pregnancy would involve risk to the life of the pregnant woman, or injury to the physical or mental health of the pregnant woman, or of any existing children of her family, is greater than if the pregnancy were terminated;

(ii) that there is a substantial risk that if the child

were born it would suffer from such physical or mental abnormalities as to be severely handicapped.

Since the passing of the Act there has been a very considerable increase in the number of women having their pregnancies terminated either in the National Health Service, private clinics, or charitable 'pregnancy advice' organizations. There has been an increasingly liberal interpretation of what is meant by 'the physical or mental health of the pregnant woman or any existing children of her family'. Consultation before agreeing to terminate a pregnancy is often minimal leading to a widely-held belief that in Britain abortion can be had on demand. So abortion becomes a kind of substitute for contraception. Pressure group organizations such as the Society for the Protection of the Unborn Child on the one hand, and the Abortion Law Reform Society on the other lead to a polarization of the argument in such a way as to make a considered judgement more difficult. Movements on either extreme try to prove their point by over-simplifying the argument. And sensational reports in the press of live foetuses being sold by nursing homes for research purposes, or of theatre staffs in hospitals hearing baby cries as an aborted foetus is taken to the incinerator, cloud the moral issue further.

The 1967 Act allowed an abortion if there were a substantial risk that if the child were born it would suffer such physical or mental abnormalities as to be seriously handicapped. To most people this would seem to be a sensible and humane regulation. It is not uncommon for a mother who has reason to believe that her child may be deformed to suffer such acute anxiety that her own health is seriously injured. Yet it is precisely when the situation is highly charged with emotion that there is the danger of coming to a hasty or facile decision. It has to be asked what right one human being has to decide whether it is in the interest of another human being to live or not to live. What is the moral situation if, on the basis of a faulty diagnosis, a foetus is aborted which had it been allowed to live would have been a perfectly normal healthy child? This is not to argue that abortion should never take place on the grounds that the child may be severely handicapped. But it does show that this is a very difficult area of moral choice, and the advocates of easier abortion often over-simplify the issue in order to make their case.

When it comes to assessing the balance between the child's life, the physical or mental health of the mother and the well-being of the other members of the family, the choice may also be very hard. To a great extent it must be a matter of medical or psychiatric opinion. There are times when abortion may be justified on these grounds. But there is need for vigilance. Just as 'mental cruelty' has in the past been used to cover a multitude of situations for procuring a divorce, so 'mental health' can be very widely interpreted as a justification for an abortion which may, in fact, be unnecessary.

What about abortion following rape? If the rights of the child are the prime consideration there would seem little argument in favour of this. The fact that a child is criminally conceived does not deny its right to be born. Yet compassion cannot always follow logic, and it may be that this is an instance where the well-being of the pregnant woman must take precedence over the life of an unborn child.

Those who believe that abortion is always wrong

43

demand nothing less than the repeal of the 1967 Act. But the danger is that this may return us to back-street and do-it-yourself abortions which made the passing of the Act appear to be so necessary twenty years ago. The demand for abortion will only be stemmed by much more effective sex education among young people, and this must include the best possible advice on contraception. But such advice must be given within the context of the moral standards which alone create a healthy and responsible society. Girls who become pregnant and whose first thought is to 'do away with the baby' need responsible advice on the moral and social as well as the medical aspects of their situation. This kind of counselling is time-consuming and is not easily available in the busy schedules of surgeries and clinics. But is is not enough for society to lay down rules and regulations and leave it at that. When the possibility of an abortion is under discussion it means that the girl, and possibly her boyfriend and her family, have become involved in a tragic situation. Neither censorious disapproval nor a speedy attempt to 'get it over and done with' can meet the deeply personal needs of that moment. There must be patient counselling in an atmosphere of care and compassion. This is a dimension which Christians must try to bring to this perplexing problem.

The control of death

A man suffers from severe brain damage as the result of an accident. For six months he is in a deep coma. His heart, breathing and digestive functions continue, but there is no sign of awareness. By being given essential nursing care he can be kept alive for a very long time. Is there any stage at which this care should be withdrawn? If a complication sets in, such as pneumonia, and the patient's condition deteriorates further, should the disease be allowed to take its course or should the patient be treated? If decisions have to be made, who makes them? The patient himself is unable to do so. The relatives may be in such an emotional state that they are unable to make any objective assessment of the situation. Even when the patient is not in a coma, pain-killing drugs may ease his situation whilst the relatives have to bear the mental agony in a state of full consciousness.

What about the doctor? Is he able to write off a case as 'hopeless' without any fear of contradiction? Severe illnesses from which patients inevitably died a generation ago can now either be controlled or cured. Even doctors may have mixed motives when making decisions. One man might be quite unconsciously glad to be rid of a difficult patient. Another might want his patient to hang on to life in order to test new drugs or techniques. He might justify his guinea pig treatment on the grounds that it could lead to discoveries which would, in future, save many lives.

The community at large may have other concerns. There is a shortage of medical staff, equipment and available hospital beds. How much skill, machinery, expense and space should be devoted to prolonging, for a short time, the life of one patient when there are so many waiting in the queue for essential medical treatment? Underlying these questions is the deeply held conviction about the 'sacredness of life'. This comes not only from the natural instinct of self-preservation, but also from the Christian religion. Does the commandment 'Thou shalt not kill' include the switching off of the life-support machine in a hopeless case? If we say 'yes' to this, we then have to ask whether the command to love our neighbour as ourselves might lead to a different answer. We cannot shirk the new powers of prolonging life or arresting death which God has given us through the skills of medical science and technology. We are called not to turn our backs on these new opportunities, but to discover how they may be used with the utmost sense of reverence and responsibility. In the last resort neither texts nor regulations can lay down precisely how these new powers should be used under every circumstance. Having laid down the basic principles of man's responsibility to God and the love he owes to his neighbour, we have to begin to evolve a working philosophy within which decisions can be made. Much will always have to be left to the discretion of the doctors. But this must also be a matter for public discussion and concern, not least among Christians who claim to see matters of life and death in the broader perspectives of eternity.

It is one thing to allow a person to die with dignity in the ordinary course of nature, but what about 'putting somebody out of their misery' at their own request when the ordinary course of nature is post-poning the inevitable death at the cost of great pain and misery? For many years there has been strong pressure to get public opinion to accept the idea of euthanasia and there have been successive attempts at legislation. In 1961 the Suicide Bill became law, making it no longer a criminal offence for a person to take his own life. But it remains an offence to 'aid, abet, counsel or procure such an act'. This meant that the doctor who in good faith acceded to the request of a patient to bring the agony of a final illness to a speedy death would be in danger of committing a crime. But this gave a new incentive to the euthanasia movement, and a bill was promoted in Parliament to make legal a form of declaration requesting the administration of euthanasia to the declarant in the event of his suffering from 'a serious physical illness or impairment reasonably thought in the patient's case to be incurable and expected to cause him severe distress or to render him incapable of rational existence'. It was recognized that there is always the danger of a death wish expressed during a temporary state of depression. To safeguard against this the proposed bill carefully defined the circumstances under which a request for euthanasia could be validly made. It would have to be signed by two witnesses who testified that its significance was understood, and who would not stand to benefit from the death. The declaration could not come into force until thirty days after it had been made, and could be revoked at any time. Euthanasia could only be administered when two physicians (one of consultant status) certified that the patient was suffering from an irremedial condition. The bill failed, and the National Voluntary Euthanasia Society attempted a new tactic. In 1979 it was renamed Exit and began to focus attention on suicide as a do-it-yourself form of euthanasia by publishing the controversial booklet *A Guide to Self Deliverance*. In spite of the interest in this publication, and increased membership, the euthanasia campaign received a severe blow when two of its leading members were found guilty of aiding and abetting suicide.

In recent years the emphasis, particularly amongst Christian people, has moved from a debate about euthanasia to a concern for the care of those who are terminally ill. The practical outcome of this concern is seen in the growing hospice movement under the inspired leadership of Dame Cicely Saunders and others. The movement focuses on the need not only to relieve pain by the use of modern drugs and good nursing, but more positively in enabling the dying to spend their last days in sympathetic and hopeful surroundings, finally to die with dignity. People usually ask 'Let me go' because they feel ill, lonely and neglected. These symptoms can be alleviated by medication and good care. Yet there is no purpose in prolonging life if an 'easy death' (that is what euthanasia means) is possible. Dame Cicely Saunders has written:

> 'We have to concern ourselves with the quality of life as well as with its length, and with the pressures imposed upon the family when we are maintaining what has become only a travesty of life. There are patients for whom chemotherapy gives great benefit, but there are others for whom it becomes increasingly irrelevant, providing more side-effects with diminishing returns. We must learn to withdraw such treatment.'

And characteristically Dame Cicely adds:

> 'It is far better to have a cup of tea given slowly on your last afternoon than to have drips and tubes in all directions.'

The care of the terminally ill, a long neglected area of medicine, is now beginning to be seen as demanding the best minds in the medical and nursing professions. For most Christians this seems of more importance than attempting to find answers to the tricky medical, social and moral questions in the euthanasia debate. Yet it may be that one day some form of voluntary euthanasia will become allowed by law. Like all our powers to control our environment and destiny, this will require human beings of a moral and spiritual maturity which we have not yet reached. In all matters of life and death man must discover how to reach a new stature. Only then can he be trusted with the powers which God is beginning to place in his hands.

QUESTIONS FOR DISCUSSION

1. What are the factors which have to be taken into account when considering whether or not doctors should have the right to give contraceptive advice to girls under sixteen? When all sides of the argument have been considered, what solution seems to you to accord most closely to a Christian concern for the needs of young people?

2. Christian opinion is divided on most of the matters discussed in the Warnock Report. What are the moral questions raised by AID, IVF, surrogate parenthood and research into embryos? Do you think that there is a clear Christian answer to any of these problems? Or must Christians agree to differ?

3. Do you think that there are circumstances in which the termination of a pregnancy must be judged the lesser of two evils? What are they? Does the present law cater for all these circumstances or does it go beyond them? How, in this complicated situation, can Christians witness to their belief in the sacredness of human life?

4. Some people believe that the time will come when euthanasia is accepted as right and humane, and will become part of the law of the land. In view of

49

the Christian belief in the providence of God and his gift of eternal life, should this be welcomed or opposed? What positive case can be made in support of both sides of the argument?

These are difficult questions because they all require a certain degree of medical knowledge. Groups would be sensible to invite an experienced doctor to join their discussion on this chapter to provide the background information they need. For question 4 the help of a practitioner in geriatrics would be particularly valuable.

Notes

1. *Test Tube Babies* (Torrance), p. 1.
2. Roman Catholic Response to the Warnock Report, para. 22.
3. *Human Fertilisation and Embryology*, para. 5.2
4. The Warnock Report, para 8.17.
5. Roman Catholic Response to the Warnock Report, para. 5.2.

For Further Reading

Doctors Talking, Norman Autton (Mowbray)
Test Tube Babies—a Christian View (Becket Publications for Order of Christian Unity)
Personal Origins (CIO Publishing)
Report of the Committee of Inquiry into Human Fertilisation and Embryology, (The Warnock Report) (HMSO)
Responses to the Warnock Report
(i) *Human Fertilisation and Embryology: The Response of the Board for Social Responsibility of the General Synod of the Church of England* published by Church House, Dean's Yard, London SW1P 3NZ.
(ii) *Response to the Warnock Report by the Catholic Bishops'*

Joint Committee on Bio-Ethical issues published by the Catholic Media Office, Ashstead Lane, Godalming, Surrey GU7 1ST.

(iii) *Test Tube Babies. Morals, Science and the Law,* Professor T. F. Torrance (Scottish Academic Press, Edinburgh)

On Dying Well: An Anglican contribution to the debate on euthanasia (CIO Publications)

3. QUESTIONS ABOUT LAW AND ORDER

Jimmy Hill, the BBC sports commentator and his two colleagues are not likely to forget that May evening in 1985 when the European Cup match between Liverpool and Juventus was scheduled to begin. They had to sit in the television studio in London watching scenes of violence in the Brussels stadium, waiting for the riot to subside and the match to start. It is not surprising that their conversation turned to the ways in which football hooliganism could be stopped. They spoke of stiffer penalties, severe imprisonment, even the return of corporal punishment. And millions of viewers sickened by the scenes they saw, must have agreed with them. There is growing public anxiety today about vandalism, violence, hooliganism and mugging. Magistrates are accused of being too lenient and 'do-gooders' are said to be more interested in the criminals than in their victims. Recorded crime has risen by 200 per cent in the last twenty years. Net losses through burglary amount to £110 million a year; the cost of car thefts is £160 million. Violence in the streets makes the elderly frightened to go out at night. Women avoid certain areas for fear of being raped. Hi-jacks and terrorist bombs, once remote possibilities, are coming nearer home. It is not only the most militant who begin to demand the return of the noose and the birch. There are increasing calls for exemplary sentences to show that crime and violence do not pay. Recently a 'football hooligan' was sentenced to life imprisonment.

The purpose of punishment

What is the purpose of punishment? It is the way in which society exacts retribution from those who have offended against its laws and customs. It is the way in which it is hoped to deter the offender from repeating his offence and to discourage others from following his example. It is a way of protecting the public by locking criminals away where they can no longer do any damage. It is the means by which it is hoped that the offender will be reformed and encouraged to turn over a new leaf by giving up his evil ways. In one way or another an effective sentence will seek to do all these things. How?

Retribution is the most natural ingredient in the popular view of punishment with its often expressed desire to 'give the thugs a dose of their own medicine'. This often leads to a recommendation of extreme measures like the judge in South Carolina who gave a rapist the option of castration instead of going to prison. *The New York Times* commented: 'Why not offer pickpockets the choice between prison and amputation, or threaten "Peeping Toms" with blindness?' In some countries penalties of this 'eye for an eye' nature are often inflicted. Although this is not part of the British judicial system, whenever a particularly horrible crime is committed the comment will be heard that 'hanging is too good for him'. Reactions such as this are a sign that society has a deep moral sense which surfaces on such occasions. Yet this is when emotion can get the better of reason. The desire 'to get our own back' may take little heed of the complex influences which cause the offender to commit his crime. There is a general suspicion of 'do-gooders' when crime and punishment are discussed, but as the sciences of psychology and sociology begin to explore criminal and anti-social behaviour, the degree of personal responsibility may be lessened and society itself find it must take some share of the blame for the crimes committed against it. In such cases, severe punishment, intended to express righteous indignation, may only confuse the issue. When punishment exceeds the limits which the indignation of the community has a right to demand, it diminishes the moral stature of those who inflict it. It is said that public executions were discontinued because they created too much sympathy for the victims about to be hung. Any punishment which oversteps the mark in vindictiveness only succeeds in deafeating its own ends. Yet we must not allow a slavish following of the latest psychological or sociological fashions to blind us to the fact of evil in man and society to which the Bible bears witness. Psychological catch-phrases can be an easy way of avoiding taking sin seriously. A stiff sentence may not only be for the public good but for the good of the offender himself. People need to be protected against themselves. Punishment must be reasonably severe to deter. Soft punishment, or a high failure rate of detection, weakens the fabric of law and order. The public remain unprotected and the criminal is free to pursue his own ends. Yet punishment, if it is too severe, may have such a hardening effect that it cancels out the deterrent factor.

Today great emphasis is rightly put on the reformative aspect of punishment. This does not please those who believe that the prime purpose of punishment is to inflict pain. Yet punishment which fails to have a concern for the future well-being of the offender and faith in the possibility of his reform is an admission of defeat. So the infliction of pain as a deterrent must be carefully weighed against its effect on the character and future potential of the criminal. The reformative aspect of punishment is of particular importance in dealing with young people who have fallen foul of the law and yet have all their lives ahead of them. About a third of offenders dealt with under the criminal justice system are under seventeen years of age. The peak age for officially recorded offending is fifteen for males and fourteen for females. About one hundred and sixty thousand juveniles each year are found guilty or cautioned for indictable offences.

The young offender

What kind of punishment is most suitable for these young offenders? What will give them the best incentive to 'go straight' in future? What will deter other young people from following their bad example? Many experiments have been tried. None has yet proved infallible. The latest form of custodial punishment for young people is to send them to a youth custody centre. These centres were set up by the Home Office in 1977. They intended to give the youngsters a 'short sharp shock'. When the Home Secretary announced the scheme he described the rigorous regime. 'From 6.45 a.m. until lights out life will be carried on at a brisk pace.' This announcement was met with prolonged applause. But does it work? A BBC film on life in one of these centres was illuminating. The regime did not seem to be particularly harsh. It just looked pointless. The authorities cut down the time given initially to drill and gymnastics because the boys came to enjoy them. Instead we saw the inmates digging the same patch of ground or scrubbing the same length of corridor. When asked what they thought about it, the boys said it was 'just boring'. Boredom is a poor punishment for young people who have generally got into trouble with the law precisely because they have found life boring. There was no evidence that those who were being punished for hooliganism or theft had changed their attitude to these crimes by the time they came to the end of their sentences. It only made them rather more determined not to be found out next time. They do not even seem to have learned this lesson for available evidence shows that however soft or hard the regime, sixty-eight per cent of these young people re-offended within a very short time.

Most of the youngsters who are sent to youth custody centres are difficult, unhappy and emotional individuals from unsatisfactory environments in areas of high unemployment. They have usually had very unsatisfactory schooling with persistent truancy, have been brought up (or neglected) in an unhappy home background, have been unable to find work on leaving school, have failed to establish satisfactory relationships with the adult world, and have found life meaningless apart from the 'kicks' provided by drugs, alcohol, group violence and other forms of delinquency. It would seem that if these offenders are to be deprived of their liberty, (and some informed opinion believes thàt they should have longer custodial sentences in some cases), the period of detention should be arranged positively in helping them to develop satisfactory relationships with mature adults and with

56

one another. They should be helped to discover within themselves possibilities of developing skills and interests which will give meaning and direction to life when their period of custody is finished. But many experts in this field believe that in many cases these objectives are most likely to be met if the young offender is not deprived of his liberty, but receives positive and disciplined treatment by order of the court in his own community. It is argued that the anti-social youngster needs to be helped to find his place within his normal community and this is not made easier if he is removed from it for a long period. This community based means of dealing with the young delinquent is still in its early days. There is still much to be discovered, and its availability in different parts of the country is patchy. But many believe that the methods being developed in these Intermediate Treatment centres (as they are called) offer the most positive way forward in helping young people who are already in trouble with the law, and those likely to be so.

Capital punishment

Whenever there is a particularly brutal murder or terrorist outrage people clamour for the return of capital punishment. Is this simply done in the spirit of retribution or can hanging (or some alternative method of execution) be justified on other grounds? The deterrent effect of capital punishment cannot be proved. It cannot be said to reform. Whenever in recent years the return of the gallows has been debated in Parliament, Christian opinion has generally come out firmly against it. In 1983 Dr John Habgood, the Archbishop of York, said:

'I believe that deliberately to kill people in cold blood—and that is what hanging is—is dehumanizing to all involved. I do not believe that hanging will in the least diminish the perils of terrorism and I believe terrorists thrive on martyrs.'

The British Council of Churches wrote to all Members of Parliament on the last occasion when this came up for debate, expressing total opposition to capital punishment saying:

'The judicial taking of life as a penalty for murder does not enhance the sacredness of human life, but further devalues it.'

The Roman Catholic bishops of England and Wales issued their own statement:

'We believe that the re-introduction of capital punishment would be damaging and dehumanizing to the whole of our society. We are not convinced that legalized killing has been shown to be an effective means of controlling violence.'

Whether the men and women who occupy the pews in our churches are as clear as their leaders on this matter is another question. But all would be in agreement with the Roman Catholic bishops when they added:

'Punishment for terrible crimes should be seen to be severe.'

Six convicted murderers in post-war Britain have killed again, either in prison or after release. Punishment must deter and the public must be protected. No penal question is more urgent than this. If capital punishment is not to be restored, what is to be meant when a man or woman is sentenced for life? British prisons are dangerously overcrowded. Statistics show that the United Kingdom imprisons a significantly higher proportion of its population than any other major country of Western Europe. In many of the older Victorian gaols the cells where the prisoner not only eats and sleeps but spends two-thirds of his day are cramped and squalid. Under such primitive conditions it is unlikely that prisons can do much more than keep 'unpleasant characters' out of the public eye for a greater or lesser period. It is hardly possible that offenders can be prepared to take their place again in normal society when they are herded together under conditions which are so unlike civilized life outside the prison walls. The situation would appear to be particularly depressing and hopeless for those sentenced to long terms of imprisonment.

Members of the Archbishop of Canterbury's Commission on Urban Priority Areas visited HM Prison in Manchester and recorded their impressions in the chapter on Law and Order in their report *Faith in the City.*

> 'On the day of our visit there were over 1,400 male adult and young offender prisoners. The prison was built in 1864 to house 774 men and 335 women. We were informed that the prison sometimes now contains 1,700 prisoners. Many cells are shared by three prisoners. Owing to the scarcity of work and educational facilities more prisoners spend the greater part of their time, and many 24 hours of the day, locked in cells. These conditions are insanitary and degrading, and we were shocked to find that they have become a normal part of a prison sentence.'

Under such circumstances, the commission argued, any attempt at the reformation of the prisoner seems a hopeless task.

> 'Although we recognise that there is little evidence for the success of attempts to make

prison a place of rehabilitation we believe that it is still our Christian duty to attempt to make it so.'

Both the Home Office and those who are concerned with the local prison service are only too aware of these problems. Within the limits imposed by the grim circumstances, governors, chaplains, social workers, educationalists and prison officers do what they can to make the best of a bad job. But the need for security, the handicap of outdated buildings, and the difficulty of bringing much variety into either prison work or leisure, make reforms almost impossible. Some attempts are being made to build places of custody where the educational and therapeutic purposes of imprisonment can be pursued, and where the physical conditions make it possible to give the prisoners intelligent and humane treatment. But this is expensive. Enlightened opinion in the prison service and elsewhere is convinced that this expenditure is essential. But what about public opinion? What about Christian opinion? As Lord Donaldson once put it: 'A nation which cares more about three hens in a cage than three men in a cell is not likely to rush into the vast sums required.'

Police and public

Sir Robert Mark, a former Commissioner of the Metropolitan Police once said that the way to reduce deliberate crime is not the severity of the sentence imposed, but the probability of being caught and convicted. If this is to be achieved a nation must have a strong and efficient police force which has the full confidence of the law-abiding general public. What should be the role of the police in a modern democratic society? The answer was given one hundred and fifty years ago by Sir Robert Mayne, a former

Metropolitan Police Commissioner. He saw three primary objects for an efficient police force:

the prevention of crime;
the protection of life and property;
the preservation of public tranquillity.

In the century and a half since then the British police have earned an enviable reputation both in this country and abroad. Many foreign tourists admire the easy way the 'bobby' can be approached to ask the time or to be shown the way. He is contrasted with the military style of many European forces, or the American 'cops' with their pistols and handcuffs hanging from their belts. James Anderton, the Chief Constable of Manchester has an even higher opinion of his calling, daring to say that policing is 'very much the sort of thing that Christ himself was doing when he was alive'.

Chief Constable Anderton is a man of deep Christian conviction. But not everyone would share his view of the police force as an army of latter-day Jesus Christs. The police continue to be admired and trusted by many, especially when they make a spectacular arrest or uncover an IRA armoury, but there can be little question that respect for the police and confidence in the way they maintain law and order has declined seriously in some parts of the country, amongst certain sections of the population, and particularly in the inner cities. The old-fashioned image of the policeman in the children's books, friendly and slow-witted, has given way to the speed cop racing down the motorway to catch the unwary, and the phalanx of officers at a football stadium or by the picket line. To many young people they are the 'pigs'. To many blacks they have become the traditional enemy. The 'bobby' on the beat has become the professional in a modern sophisticated police force.

The tools of his trade are the panda car, the two-way radio, the radar equipment. His search for the criminal is backed up by the latest computer technology. With the sanction of the Home Secretary he has in reserve an armoury of CS gas canisters, plastic bullets and water cannon. He can be mobilized into highly trained units of a para-military nature such as the Special Patrol Group and the Anti-terrorist Squad. Present day violence, organized crime, terrorism, mass demonstrations and football hooliganism, all, he claims, need to be met by a new kind of police force with maximum mobility, instant communication and sophisticated technology. In no other way can the modern criminal be caught and the public protected.

There is good reason for this new police professionalism. Yet there is also anxiety. Is the emphasis today placed more on catching the criminal than on the protection of the public? Does police mobility put them out of touch with the public they are there to serve? In a democracy police must operate with the consent of the people who pay for their services through taxation. Those who provide the cash do not have the right to dictate the operational methods the police must employ. That is a matter of professional judgement. But the public must have confidence in the powers which are delegated to the police, understand fully what those powers are, and approve of the ways in which they are used. Without this confidence and consent, trust between police and public is in jeopardy, and the moral fibre of society weakened.

In recent years the police in Britain have found themselves more and more called upon to maintain law and order at political demonstrations and industrial disputes. Not only does this raise many practical problems about policing methods, it also poses difficult moral questions about the relationship between freedom and discipline in our permissive society. In Britain we have always prided ourselves on freedom of speech and protest and the right to demonstrate. But in recent years mass marches and demonstrations have from time to time led to serious public disorder. People expect to be protected against being bullied, obstructed, intimidated. How can that protection be afforded them by law without infringing people's right to meet and express their views in peaceful yet sometimes massive demonstrations? What powers should the police be given to maintain both civil rights and public order? A Government White Paper published in May 1985 proposed giving the police wider control over public demonstrations. Marches would require seven days' notice, with the exception of certain religious and traditional processions. The police would have discretionary powers to impose conditions on organizers of outdoor assemblies if there was a likelihood of serious public disorder or disruption to the local community. Recent events have suggested the need for this kind of control. Yet there is anxiety that the police will find themselves having to make political decisions as they give or withhold permission for the organization of certain events. *The Guardian* newspaper, describing these proposals as a 'nasty piece of work' said that any attempt by Government to extend police powers and to reduce the freedom of protest would have to be viewed with suspicion. Yet can too high a price be paid for that freedom? Are there limits which should not be over-stepped? How can the right balance be found?

Many new questions have arisen from the massive deployment of the police in the national miners' strike in 1984–85. Press and television concentrated on the pits where police and pickets were involved in violent confrontation. The many other areas where picketing was on a modest and orderly scale did not hit the headlines. But in some places violence bred violence on both sides. As an inquiry set up by the National Council for Civil Liberties reported:

'We have been shocked both by the sight of pickets throwing missiles and of vehicles overturned and set alight, and by the sight of police officers on horseback charging into crowds and wielding batons.'[1]

The police had a hard task safeguarding those miners who wished to continue working. Going to work during a strike is a lawful activity and they had every right to expect protection for themselves and for their families in the face of violence, threats, physical obstruction and intimidation from their fellow miners on strike. On the other hand, the response to large-scale picketing by an equally massive police presence had a knock-on effect which probably further aggravated the situation. The setting up of road blocks to prevent flying pickets coming from a distance was an extension of doubtful legality of powers normally reserved for catching escaped prisoners or perpetrators of serious offences. The police were under very considerable strain during the long months of the strike, particularly as most of them were drafted to places far away from home, living in uncomfortable billets and working long hours. It is not surprising that some of them overreacted, damaging property and frightening residents in their pursuit of pickets. A bright moment in this dark dispute was when the Chief Constable of South Yorkshire visited the colliery village of Grimethorpe and publicly apologized to the inhabitants for police excesses. Speaking in a debate in the House of Lords on policing the Bishop of Gloucester said:

'Everything possible should be done to eradicate

anything which would drive further wedges of misunderstanding and hostility between policemen and the most ordinary citizens, even the less well behaved ones, and especially the vulnerable, the fearful and the inarticulate.'

Community policing

In reaction to the disappearance of the old-fashioned 'bobby' on the beat, the new concept of community policing is being developed. This demands that a police officer is on his own patch long enough to get to know the people and their problems and to be known by them. It takes time for a community-based constable to build up a good knowledge of his area, and to form constructive relationships. It is not spectacular work and does not command a high place in policing priorities. But its importance has been stressed by the Archbishop of Canterbury:

'A policing style has to be negotiated with the local community to provide the basis for the greatest possible co-operation in the vitally important matter of maintaining social order and respect for the law.'

The community constable is the local face of the police. The whole force is judged by the impression he makes. If he is to earn mutual trust and respect he must remain in the area for a number of years. He must be well known in schools, youth clubs and local organizations. He must work closely with teachers, social workers, planners, councillors and the clergy. His friendly contact with local residents is particularly important in inner city areas, especially where there are considerable numbers of people of African, Caribbean, or Asian origin. There is a genuine fear that the attitude of some police is that if a man is black he is likely to be a criminal. After the Brixton riots Lord Scarman criticized the police for failing to adapt their methods to a multi-racial society. Some police officers (like some of the general public) are racist in outlook, and this attitude can harm the reputation of the whole constabulary. Others approach black people with an insensitivity which comes more from fear or ignorance than from racial prejudice. It is a matter of urgency that police colleges should include courses on race community relations, and provide police cadets with the opportunity of meeting and talking face to face with representatives of ethnic minority groups. Local clergy and community workers could give the police considerable assistance here. They know well the areas in which they serve, and are able to see local problems in a different perspective from those whose job it is to uphold the law and apprehend those who transgress it.

Police accountability

The corollary to all this emphasis on community policing is that the police themselves must be more willing to find ways of establishing good relationships with the public. They must learn to take people more into their confidence, listen to what they have to say, and be ready to take criticism seriously. This is what many police officers are unwilling to do. They see themselves as a self-sufficient professional organization entrusted by society with the task of enforcing the law and bringing criminals to justice. Sir David McNee, a former Metropolitan Police Commissioner once said to his critics, 'Get off our backs and allow us to get on with our job!' John Alderson, former Chief Constable of Devon and Cornwall took a different view. He described the problem of a traditional autocratic and hierarchical body like the police adjusting itself to a democratic society in which increasingly ordinary people were demanding a voice in decision making:

> 'When the mass of people have tasted the permissiveness formerly enjoyed by a few, they are unlikely to put up with old-fashioned police authoritarianism. This, in turn, may lead the police in a non-stratified society to retreat behind their legal barricades, only venturing forth to deal with clear, provable, criminal acts. This kind of thing, inducing as it does a legalistic, reactionary, technological style of policing, only serves to widen the gulf between the bemused police and a truculent public. The situation in turn becomes compounded by misunderstanding, suspicion, and hostility, making the job of the police more difficult to do and to understand.'[2]

The tension between the police and those they are called to serve becomes more obvious when someone wishes to make a complaint against the police for what they consider to have been unfair treatment. This is a constant cause for resentment. At present complaints are dealt with by the police themselves, in more serious cases calling in the help of a senior officer from another police district. Inevitably these internal investigations, however scrupulously conducted, raise doubts about their impartiality, and some chief officers are sympathetic to this feeling of anxiety. Others are convinced of the impartiality of the existing system and feel that those who are agitating for change are trouble-makers intent on stirring up anti-police feeling. But following the Brixton riots Lord Scarman called for an entirely independent system of dealing with complaints against the police, and strong support has come from the British Council of

Churches. There is also a need to remove fear (founded or unfounded) that those who come forward with complaints are black-listed by the police and may become subject to harassment or intimidation.

Margaret Simey, for many years a much respected local councillor in Liverpool and chairman of the Merseyside Police Authority, has written persuasively on the need for the police to be ultimately accountable to the public:

> 'The police can be authorized to enforce the law and be given far reaching powers to do so, but the final responsibility, that of ensuring that they do so impartially and efficiently and in accordance with the law and the wishes of the people, must remain with the people.'[3]

In 1964 the Police Act replaced the old watch committees with Police Authorities. The membership of these bodies consists of two-thirds local councillors and one-third magistrates. Although they have a right to demand reports from the Chief Constable, he has a right to refuse if he thinks that a report 'would contain information which in the public interest ought not to be disclosed or is not needed for the discharge of the function of the Police Authority'. In a number of areas there is considerable tension between the Authority and the Chief Constable who resists what he thinks to be political interference in his work. Sir Kenneth Newman, the Metropolitan Police Commissioner has warned of the 'danger of control by an ideology rather than the public good'. The Chief Constable of Greater Manchester called for the abolition of all police authorities declaring that 'accountability is a fashionable term used by those who wish to give orders to the police'.

Another of Lord Scarman's proposals after Brixton was the setting up of Police Liaison Committees where local representatives could discuss policy with senior officers. Several police forces in different parts of the country have established voluntary community liaison schemes, and local churches or councils of churches are taking some share in them. Here is a valuable opportunity for church congregations to become involved through carefully chosen representatives in the problems and concerns of policing in their own area and to make a constructive contribution. The British Council of Churches has urged that if the local church has the opportunity of being represented on a committee of this kind, the man or woman chosen must have a wide local knowledge, be ready to listen, and be prepared to be non-partisan whatever their political viewpoint. It is also essential that through their representative the work of the liaison committee should be made known to the churches in the area. There are other more informal ways in which contacts between the local churches and the local police can be made, and these should be explored. We need not only an effective police force for the maintaining of law and order but also a concerned and, where necessary, critical public. As Margaret Simey has written:

'Until we can work out a sophisticated and civilized partnership between police and people, the future of policing by consent is indeed in doubt.'[4]

To work to this end is a Christian responsibility.

Victim support

It is sometimes said that people are more interested in the criminal than in their victims. The whole focus of the criminal justice system is on catching, trying and punishing the offender. There is much less knowledge or interest in what crime does to the victims, and little practical help given to those who suffer at the hands of a criminal. Victims often feel neglected by their neighbours or the communities in which they live. Part of the shock may come from the feeling that 'nobody cares about me'. Part of the often very necessary healing process is the knowledge that 'somebody does care'. The director of the National Association of Victims' Support Schemes has written:

> 'Just as an offer of friendship and support can help to balance the potentially devastating effect of crime on individuals, so everyone who is worried about the prospect of crime should know equally that there is an increasing number of people who are prepared to give their time and effort unstintingly in an attempt to put things right.'5

The first victims' support scheme was started in Bristol in 1974. Now there are two hundred and fifty schemes up and down the country. There are 6,000 volunteers helping more than 125,000 victims to recover from the shock of burglary, violence, criminal damage and other offences ranging from the trauma of sexual assault to the shock many feel after an intruder has been rummaging about in their homes. Some need support over a long period if they are to regain their confidence. As distressing as the crime itself, may be the prolonged court proceedings which follow, especially if the victim is required as a witness. Each victim support scheme is designed to offer maximum support and practical assistance to individuals and families suffering distress or inconvenience as a result of crime. Each scheme develops according to the local situation, and involves as wide a range of people whose experience can be of service. The key person in the scheme is called the co-ordinator who receives referrals (usually from the police) and who selects the appropriate visitor to call on the victim and discover what particular help is required.

Many of the visitors have had previous experience in such fields as medical or social work, or religious counselling. Others, equally essential, are just good neighbours. All go through a process of selection and training which involves co-operation with the churches, police, hospitals and voluntary bodies which specialize in such personal tragedies as rape or bereavement. In some areas special attention has to be given to the effect of racially-motivated crime.

These teams of volunteers visit the victim at home as soon as possible after referral. Relations, doctors, neighbours and the local churches may be called to assist. Local clubs may be contacted to provide practical help and appointments for professional advice may be made with solicitors, crime prevention and insurance specialists and other experts known to the scheme. People in need of long term care may be referred to such agencies as the social services, Age Concern, or the WRVS.

Financial help for victims is now available through government schemes. Since 1964 state compensation has also been available to victims of criminal injury. Many feel that the offenders themselves should be made responsible either by being ordered to pay compensation if they have the means, or, in appropriate cases, to give personal service to those against whom they have offended. For the criminal to be brought face to face with the human consequences of his crime might under certain circumstances be of benefit not only to the offender but also to the offended against. But this does not remove the necessity of further development in Victim Support Schemes. This service to those in special and sudden need is still in its early stages and there is much to be learned. Here is a field of commitment in which local churches and individual Christians can have a major part to play.

Civil disobedience

Are there any occasions when a Christian may come to the conclusion in good conscience that not only may it be right to break the law, but that it is his duty to do so? This is becoming a matter of urgent debate among many Christian people in Britain today. It is easy to applaud law-breaking in the heroes of the past such as Mahatma Gandhi, Martin Luther King or Dietrich Bonhoeffer. It is also easy to rejoice at the courage of our fellow Christians in Poland or South Africa who dare to face the consequence of civil disobedience for the sake of freedom and justice. Such men and women must find it hard to accept Paul's advice to the people of Rome as if it were the last word to be said on the subject. Is it true of the communist government in Poland or of the government upholding apartheid in South Africa that:

> 'there is no authority but by act of God, and the existing authorities are instituted by him, consequently anyone who rebels against authority is resisting a divine institution'?[6]

Those who accept these words as 'gospel' will remain convinced that civil disobedience is always against the will of God. But many of the saints now honoured in the Church calendar thought and acted otherwise, and faced the consequences. Jesus himself suffered the penalty reserved for those committing crimes against the government of the day. Peter and John, arrested by the police and ordered by the magistrates to refrain from teaching in public boldly replied: 'Is it right in God's eyes for us to obey you rather than God?'

At the time of the trial of Dr Beyers Naude in South Africa which resulted in his imprisonment, the South African Christian Institute (since banned) issued a statement:

'Civil disobedience is an act of protest by Christians on the grounds of Christian conscience. It is only permitted when authority expects of them an un-christian deed. When a government deviates from the Gospel the Christian is bound by his conscience to resist it. Even if this results in breaking the law, it has to be done because God's will must be maintained above the law of man.'

But Great Britain is not Poland or South Africa. We live in a democratic country. The ballot box is open to all. If we dislike the Government we can work towards putting it out of power. For many Christians these arguments are strong enough to maintain that in our situation civil disobedience cannot be justified on moral grounds. They suspect some of the militant protest movements which attract a wide diversity of strange fellow-travellers from many different points of view and with many different motives. The Christian witness can easily become blurred and distorted. What is intended to be non-violent protest can lead to violent confrontation with the police. Should Christians be careful about the company they keep? But others are not convinced by these arguments, and believe that Christians must be prepared to take risks for the sake of conscience, including risks to their own reputation.

Large numbers of Christian people in Britain today are totally opposed to the use of nuclear weapons and are doubtful about the morality, as well as the effectiveness, of the nuclear deterrent. The majority opinion both in Parliament, in the nation and even in the Church may not agree with them. But they hold strongly to their conviction, and believe that the only way in which they can get a hearing for their point of view is by public protest, mass demonstration and non-violent action, even if this may bring them into conflict with the law. Many of those who have taken part in anti-nuclear demonstrations at Greenham Common or Molesworth, and have appeared before the magistrates in consequence, claim that the driving force behind their protest, and the courage and determination to pursue it, springs from their Christian conviction. For the same reason, members of the Society of Friends and others have taken part in the Peace Tax Campaign. Their concern is that forty-five per cent of their income tax is used to maintain a nuclear defence policy to which they are in conscience opposed. They have requested that this proportion of their tax payment should be diverted into a special 'non-armaments fund'. The tax authorities have refused on the grounds that Parliament has the duty to levy taxes and to decide how they are to be used. Those who persist in this campaign could incur penalties for tax evasion.

In the 1914–18 war many pacifists suffered harsh imprisonment for refusing to take up arms. The courageous stand they took eventually became accepted as a right to conscientious objection. During the Vietnam war many American students tore up their draft cards and refused to accept conscription because they believed that their country was engaged in an unjust war. The Churches, and especially the chaplains in universities and colleges, gave them strong support.

This debate will be with us for a long time, and Christians should not evade it just because the question of civil disobedience and law-breaking for conscience' sake is a very difficult one. In national church synods, in local congregations and even in Christian families, opinion will be deeply divided. Both sides of the argument must continue to test their convictions with all possible honesty, and try to listen carefully to the deeply-held convictions of those with whom they disagree. The Christian community should provide the setting for a humble exchange of views in which listening is always as important as speaking, and the readiness to be proved wrong as essential as the courage to hold to convictions.

QUESTIONS FOR DISCUSSION

1. What does the Christian understanding of the way God deals with us tell us about the way we should treat those who have offended against their fellow men?

2. Consider, in the light of the Christian command to love your neighbour (which includes offenders), the respective merits of imprisonment and fines. Should greater use be made of other penalties such as community service, suspended sentences, weekend custody and disqualifications?

3. Under what circumstances, if any, is it a Christian duty to break the law? Can you give specific instances when this might be applicable in your own country?

4. Why do you think there has been a deterioration in police-public relations? What steps can be taken to improve the situation? Assuming that good relationships are essential for the moral health of the

community, what role can the Church play in this matter?

5. What steps have been taken, or ought to be taken, in your locality to help the victims of crime?

Useful help in discussing these questions could be had by inviting to your group a representative of the police, probation service, magistracy, or someone dealing particularly with young offenders in youth custody or intermediate treatment schemes.

Notes

1. *Civil Liberties and the Miners' Dispute,* para. 3.8.
2. *Policing Freedom,* page 4.
3. *Government by Consent,* page 18.
4. op. cit. page 15.
5. Further information from the National Association of Victims' Support Schemes, 34 Electric Lane, Brixton, London SW9.
6. Romans 13. 1–6.
7. Acts. 4. 19–20.

For Further Reading

Policing Freedom, John Alderson (Macdonald and Evans)
Policing in a Democratic Society (General Synod Board for Social Responsibility, Church House, Dean's Yard, London SW1P 3NZ)
Government by Consent, Margaret Simey (Bedford Square Press/NCVO)
Civil Liberties and the Miners' Dispute (National Council of Civil Liberties)

4. QUESTIONS ABOUT RACE AND NATIONALITY

A multi-racial society

A black South African Methodist minister working in England wrote to the *Methodist Recorder*:

> 'I have been a victim of racism all my life in South Africa but my most humiliating experiences have been here within the Church in Britain.'

Such a statement comes as a shock. The challenge of Jesus Christ is seldom tested so accurately as by the attitude of his followers to people of different races. Evidence suggests that many Christians in the British Isles fail that test.

For many decades Britain has been a multi-racial country. There are now over two million coloured immigrants in Britain; seventy per cent of them live in Greater London, the West Midlands, Merseyside, Tyne and Wear and West Yorkshire. Many of them are British born; some are three generations removed from the relatives who first came here from overseas. Most no longer like to think of themselves as immigrants. They are British nationals, often speaking with an accent more typical of the district where they live than of their country of origin. The largest group is from West Indies and Guyana, many of them descended from African slaves who were shipped to the Caribbean by their English masters. At first it was largely skilled men who came to Britain to meet demands for labour. Many of the young women entered the nursing profession. It is said that the National Health Service could not have survived without them. The West Indians like to settle together in the same neighbourhood, and are glad to enter quickly into the British way of life joining churches, trade unions and political parties. But bad housing, unemployment and racial discrimination have often prevented them from taking as full a part in the life of the community as they would wish.

Indians and Pakistanis form another large group. Most of the Indians are Sikhs and are amongst the best organized of the ethnic minority groups, though their women are often reluctant to speak English. Other Indians are Hindus. Some become doctors, or achieve other professions, but many with educated or middle class backgrounds have to be content with manual work—if they can get work at all. The Pakistanis are Muslims, many are unmarried. Like other immigrants they are often heard to be critical of the moral permissiveness of British society, and especially of what they consider to be our lax way of bringing up children. Among the smaller ethnic minority groups are the closely-knit Chinese communities which are of long standing in some of our cities. The most recent arrivals are the Vietnamese 'boat people' who fled their country in South East Asia, and have settled (with mixed success) in different parts of the country. But the flow of immigrants coming here has now become a trickle following the immigration policies of successive governments.

Initially all these visitors from overseas were welcomed with open arms because we needed them to help in the reconstruction of our national economy after the war. Today the situation is different. In areas of high unemployment the chance of a black person getting a job is even more remote than for a white person. When substantial immigration was taking place in the sixties people were being encouraged to move out from the city centres into the new housing estates where there were better facilities. But the immigrants were not eligible for these new houses under the length of residence regulations, and they had to buy or rent the less expensive properties with the least amenities in the decaying inner cities. So the ghettos like Brixton in London, Toxteth in Liverpool, Moss Side in Manchester, St Paul's in Bristol and Handsworth in Birmingham came into being. The black presence in Britain was coming to be resented. Politicians like Enoch Powell predicted racial trouble ahead, and threatened 'rivers of blood' if the number of immigrants was not sharply reduced. There was a growing incidence of abuse, ridicule, harassment, vandalism and physical assault levelled against the ethnic minorities. Racist groups like the National Movement organized campaigns of hatred. And a great number of 'decent' people (including church members) stood by and said nothing, or perhaps did not even notice what was happening. In a speech to the Birmingham Community Relations Council Dr Robert Runcie, the Archbishop of Canterbury, said:

> 'As I travel round the country I still frequently meet suburban-dwelling decision makers who claim that there is no race problem in their leafy avenues, when their own lack of urgency and lack of conviction that measures have to be taken to

redress racial disadvantage is itself a major contribution to the problem.'[1]

The truth is that Britain is a racist society.

Racism and the Churches

To the Christian this must be deeply disturbing for it denies much of what lies at the heart of the Gospel. A 'Wayside Pulpit' posted outside a Church once declared 'God is colour blind'. The message was well-intentioned, but it was a travesty of the truth. Would God have created such a rich diversity within the human race of colour and culture were it of no significance? The privilege of living in a multi-racial society is to discover the rich kaleidoscope of the many colours which together make up mankind. The writer of Revelation had a vision of the fulfilment of God's purpose in the new Jerusalem when he saw 'a vast throng which no one could count, from every nation, of all tribes, peoples and languages.'[2] But God's plan is foiled by human sin. The diversity which should bring such a rich harmony within the unity of one family becomes the cause of division, prejudice and suspicion. Jesus came to do away with division and to create unity out of the rich plurality. He gave his life to restore the common humanity of all people created by God. At a world consultation in 1980 the World Council of Churches declared:

'Every human being created in the image of God is a person for whom Christ died. Racism, which is the use of a person's racial origin to determine a person's value, is an assault on Christ's values, and a rejection of his sacrifice.'

In a remarkable essay in a symposium on *Theology and Racism,* John Austin Baker, the Bishop of Salisbury, sks what he called 'this unhappy question'. Given the clear teaching of the Bible, 'Why is it that Christianity more than any other of the world's religions has succumbed to the racist disease?'[3] He traces the answer to his own question back to the New Testament. He points out how in St John's Gospel 'The Jews' is always used as a pejorative term. How in St Matthew's account of the Passion 'great efforts are made to show that the blame for the death of Jesus rests on the Jews, the leaders principally, but also on all the people'. How in the Acts of the Apostles 'the vast majority of the Jews are presented as utterly bigoted and unscrupulous in their hostility to and persecution of Christians'. Today many scholars believe that the death of Jesus was instigated primarily by the Roman Imperial government as a political execution, and that it was only a small group of Jewish leaders who found it expedient to collaborate with their Roman masters. The great mass of Jewish people were not involved. But when the Gospels came to be written the Church had spread into many parts of the Roman Empire, and it was more prudent for its survival to put the blame for the death of Jesus primarily on the Jews (with whom the Christians were now in conflict) than on the Roman authorities. But whatever the precise cause, anti-semitism has been one of the blots on Christian history, though, as events have tragically shown in this century, the persecution of Jews is not exclusively a Christian habit.

In any discussion on Christianity and racism today the responsibility of Christian people to try to understand and appreciate their Jewish neighbours is of great importance. In the Old Testament Scriptures and in many aspects of our worship, tradition, and theology, we share a common root. Where there is a local branch of the Council of Christians and Jews, it should be given the fullest support. Where there is a local synagogue useful contact can be made with the rabbi or Jewish leaders to arrange mutual visits, study and discussion sessions and social gatherings. The two-way process can be of real benefit to both Christians and Jews. As Pope John Paul II has said 'to assess carefully the faith and religious life of the Jewish people as they are professed and practised still today, can greatly help us to understand better certain aspects of the life of the Church'.[4]

Christianity and other faiths

Whenever we are able to come close to people of other faiths and cultures our own horizons are widened. Some Christians are fearful lest they should be contaminated by contact with other religions in our multi-faith society, but the Archbishop of Canterbury does not agree:

> 'The presence of ethnic groups with their different religious traditions has given new breadth and generosity to our vision of the brotherhood of man and the fatherhood of God. Also, in consequent dialogue between the faiths the result, in my experience, has been far from a dilution of faith, but rather a fresh grasp of what is particular and precious about Christianity alongside a growth of knowledge of and a respect for other religious traditions.'[5]

Church congregations which meet for worship in parts of the country where many people of different races and cultures live have a particular responsibility to demonstrate in practice that Christians are concerned to combat racism and to build racial harmony.

But every individual Christian has a part to play. We can begin by daring to face up to the racist feelings that most of us have deep down inside ourselves, and talking with other people about how this can be overcome. We can invite black people and other racial minorities to tell us frankly about their experience of living in a predominantly white society. We can make certain that our children, both at school and in church, understand something of the ways of people whose faces are a different colour from their own. Some school books, children's story books, and the more old-fashioned Sunday school and missionary literature retain traces of a former colonial and patronizing outlook. We should show more concern about the situation in our inner city areas where blacks and whites share the same problems of poverty, bad housing and social disadvantage. We can learn to be sensitive to and active on behalf of any cases of racial discrimination in employment or housing which come to our attention in our own district. We can ensure that the abolition of all racial discrimination has an essential place in our proclamation of the Gospel. We can join forces with other bodies in our community who are working for racial harmony. We can attempt, where possible, to get adequate representation of minorities on church councils, deanery, diocesan or district synods, ecumenical bodies, school governors and similar bodies. At present very few people of African or Asian origin have been ordained into the ministry of the Church of England, though the consecration, in July 1985, of Wilfred Wood as Bishop of Croydon, the first black man to become a bishop in England, gives hope for the future. And we should be aware of all moves taken by the Churches in our country and overseas to oppose discrimination

and to promote justice and equality for all men and
women whatever their colour, nationality or race.

Race and the Law

The promotion of good race relations is not only a
concern of the Churches. It is also a national responsibility. In 1965 the Race Relations Act sought for the
first time to make racial discrimination and incite-
ment to racial hatred offences against the law. Two
years later further legislation made discrimination
unlawful in employment, housing and education. In
1976 a third Race Relations Act brought into being
the Commission for Racial Equality.[6] This govern-
ment-sponsored body, which is often much criticized,
is concerned with the investigation of complaints of
discrimination and exposing ways in which discrimination occurs. It monitors the development of race
relations laws in such areas as employment, housing,
education, local government, the police and the social
services. It attempts to break down prejudice and
intolerance through public education, conferences
and literature. It provides grants and practical help to
local community relations councils which now
number over a hundred. These local councils mani-
fest a wide variety of concerns including health and
welfare, human rights, youth and education, housing
and employment, social and cultural questions, religious education and legal matters. It is fashionable in
some quarters to denigrate what is sometimes dispar-
agingly called 'the race relations industry' by claiming
that the councils and the law itself creates rather than
heals racial disharmony. This is not true. Local community relation councils need all the encouragement
and practical help they can get, and the churches

have a special responsibility here—one that they do not always take seriously.

It is over twenty years since the first Race Relations Act came into force. Some progress has been made, but there is cause for much disappointment. The most recent report of the Commission for Racial Equality (June 1985) confesses that ethnic minorities in this country still suffer severe disadvantages and that 'serious inequalities, to which discrimination on racial grounds has contributed, persist in employment, housing, education and other services'. The report ends with an urgent plea.

'In tackling disadvantage and discrimination we are tackling problems some of which have roots in centuries-old prejudices that are endemic in our society. No one could reasonably have supposed that these problems would be solved in two decades. But how long will they take to solve in future? We need to make faster progress. There is nothing inevitable about achieving improvements in race relations. Unless there is active commitment from everyone in a position of power and authority, everyone who can choose between allowing discrimination to continue and actively to stop it, we may find that at the end of another two decades the measure of disadvantage and inequality of opportunity will tell no better story than they do today. That would be tragic.'

The British Churches play their part in this struggle through the social responsibility boards of the denominations, and together through the work of the Community and Race Relations Unit of the British Council of Churches.[7] This is a concern which also must be reflected in the worship and witness of every local church congregation, and in the thinking of every individual Christian.

Immigration

The law not only attempts to improve the quality of race relations in the country, it also determines who may or may not cross our frontiers to make their home here. Under the British Nationality Act of 1948 anyone born in a colony of the Empire was automatically a citizen of the United Kingdom. As late as 1963 British subjects from anywhere in the world could come to live and work in the United Kingdom without restriction. During the next ten years both Conservative and Labour governments passed a series of immigration laws which severely restricted the entry of British subjects who previously had an absolute right to come here. After 1971 entry of United Kingdom citizens from former colonies was limited to those whose fathers or grandfathers were born here. So the law, in practice, gave right of entry and freedom to work to millions of white immigrants from commonwealth countries. But for black people from the Caribbean, Africa and the Indian sub-continent it became increasingly difficult to gain entry, even if other members of their family had already settled here. Asians resident in East Africa who had been allowed to keep United Kingdom citizenship because they had been excluded from citizenship of their original country when it achieved independent status, found that when they wished to move to Great Britain the door was closed to them. They became refugees in their adopted African homes or (if they were able) came into this country as illegal immigrants. Some few were admitted each year on a voucher system.

This was increased when Great Britain was taken to the European Court of Human Rights charged with being guilty of 'inhuman and degrading treatment of its own nationals'. There have been occasions when the voucher system has been waived as when the Ugandan Asians were suddenly expelled by Idi Amin, and when the British Government agreed to take a quota of Vietnamese 'boat people' refugees. But today very few black immigrants are allowed to enter this country. British nationals in India may have to wait for several years before being allowed to enter the United Kingdom. The Home Office justifies this system: 'The effective way to deal with the problem is by a steady flow which does not raise justifiably or unjustifiably public apprehension.'

Other aspects of immigration legislation which have been criticized by the Churches include the denial of the right of fiancés or spouses to join their partners already resident in this country, the status of children born in this country now that the tradition of citizenship by place of birth has been abandoned, the increasing difficulty and expense of making a formal application for British citizenship, and the deportation of people who have lived here for several years, put down roots, and have found their place in the local community, but are technically illegal immigrants. It is difficult not to see racist tendencies in the law as it stands and in the heartless way in which it is sometimes applied. Every country must have regulations controlling immigration, but the motives which lie behind those regulations need very careful examination. A statement issued in 1979 by the Roman Catholic bishops of England and Wales insisted that:

'Any new nationality law should state as a matter

of principle that our national identity is multi-racial, thereby avoiding any potentially racialist conception of national identity which could lead to racial discrimination in the law as its interpretation.'[8]

The Church of England Board for Social Responsibility took up the same theme in a paper on the 1981 Nationality Act. In criticizing the concept of patriality (the limiting of immigration permits to those United Kingdom citizens with parents or grandparents born in this country) it declared:

'The use of patriality in citizenship undermines a basic principle of the equal dignity and status under the law of all members of the community irrespective of race or origin. It is necessary to guard citizenship and entry laws against any charge of discrimination on the basis of race or sex. It is our belief that the present laws do not keep within those boundaries.'

There are some people who, in Margaret Thatcher's words, have a 'fear of being swamped'. There are others, more extreme in their opinions, who dislike foreigners, especially if they are black, and would like them all to be sent back to the places from which they or their forbears came. The Archbishop of Canterbury has warned against views of this sort:

'Britain is inescapably a multi-racial country. Any talk of repatriating people who have sometimes lived here for more than two generations and who are no longer welcome in their countries of origin is a dangerous fantasy. We are, in fact, a multi-racial society, and the choice we have is between working to make the fact a matter of pride and celebration, or drifting into a situation where the fact is a matter of lament and despair.'[9]

Christian men and women, by virtue of the fact that they are members of a great international society, the Church of Jesus Christ, should always approach the fact of living in a multi-racial society not first and foremost as a problem but as an opportunity and privilege to be grasped.

Racism in the world

In 1981 the Social Responsibility Board of the Church of England invited fifty men and women to meet for three days in Leicester to consider the role of the Church in the struggle for racial justice. Although the recommendations which emerged had no official status, and not all participants agreed with every detail in the published report, they provided a useful guide to an informed body of Christian opinion. After five years their conclusions are still relevant and the recommendations continue to be urgent. Much of the report focuses on the practical implications of the Church here is part of the world-wide Church, and as inequality. But its concluding pages point beyond our own domestic scene to international racism. Our Church here is part of the world-wide Church, and as a former 'sending Church' in the days of missionary expansion, we still have strong links with Christians in most parts of the world. The Churches in Britain were closely associated with the growth of the British empire, and therefore must have a particular concern for the life and witness of their fellow Christians, especially in Africa and Asia, in this post-colonial era. The Leicester consultation drew particular attention to two areas which continue to arouse considerable anxiety and controversy—our relationship with South Africa and the World Council of Churches' Programme to Combat Racism.

In opposition to legalized racism in South Africa a number of points were raised as a matter of urgency:

— declaring as a basic tenet of Anglican faith that the doctrine and practice of apartheid is contrary to the gospel of Christ.
— supporting the movements for independence such as the African National Congress and SWAPO.
— disengaging economically from South Africa; withdrawing from banks which make loans to the South African Government and disinvesting from companies with subsidiaries in South Africa.
— supporting initiatives for economic sanctions.
— encouraging Christian entertainers and sports personalities not to compete in South Africa, or against South African opposites.[10]

Much has happened in the worsening situation in South Africa since these words were written in Leicester five years ago. Nor is it yet agreed among Christians that these recommendations represent the most effective line of action to be taken. In any discussion the basic question has to be asked and (if possible) answered: what policies will be of greatest value to the black majority in South Africa in their struggle for justice and civil rights? Many of them, such as Bishop Desmond Tutu, advocate disinvestment and sanctions because, even though this may cause suffering for the black population in the short run, this will hasten the day of freedom. Those who resist economic sanctions and financial boycotts convince themselves that this is in the best interest of South Africa as a whole. It is not easy to ascertain the true facts, and it is more than easy to decide on policies for South Africa which advance our own interests here at home. In any discussion on racism our own motives need the closest examination. Such an examination is a Christian duty.

The other area of controversy surrounds the Programme to Combat Racism. When the World Council of Churches was formed forty years ago, its membership came predominantly from Europe, North America and the former colonies and dominions. Its discussions were characteristic of those which most interested theologians and ecclesiastics from western countries. Today the situation is very different. Former missionary churches in Africa and Asia are now independent of the old missionary societies and church bodies. They now sit in the World Council of Churches in their own right and with an equal voice. They are impatient of the old academic talk about freedom, justice and equality for they have to face these things in practical and difficult ways as citizens of the developing world. The World Council of Churches has issued some thirty splendid statements about racial equality. The new Churches demanded deeds as well as words. So in 1969 the World Council agreed to provide a more practical backing for those striving for racial justice by creating a special fund for distribution to organizations of oppressed racial groups or to organizations supporting the victims of racial injustice. The Council called upon its member Churches 'to move beyond charity grants and traditional programming to relevant and sacrificial action leading to new relationships of dignity and justice among all men, and to become agents of the radical reconstruction of society.' Some of the grants were for organizations such as the Patriotic Front in Zimbabwe and the Frelimos in Mozambique and others committed to the armed struggle. The grants were specifically given for humanitarian purposes, food, health, social, educational, and agricultural programmes. A World Council of Churches spokesman tried to make this clear:

> The Council is not endorsing violence any more than an army chaplain endorses the bullets of the soldiers he serves. The World Council of Churches' commitment to non-violent change is clear. But this does not mean it must desert those in need of humanitarian support when their struggle turns violent.'

The Programme to Combat Racism was widely criticized, particularly in the secular press. Headlines appeared accusing the Church of 'encouraging violence', 'supporting terrorists' and 'Church money for guerillas'. A few Churches resigned their membership of the World Council, and the General Synod of the Church of England reduced its contribution to the World Council by a token £1,000 in protest. Only a very small number of grants are given to projects of a controversial nature. The money is placed in a special fund to which member churches are invited to contribute. Neither the Church of England nor Christian Aid contribute to the fund, though many individual Christians do so with a clear conscience, and some Churches (like the Methodists) encourage them to do this. The Leicester consultation urged the Church of England to contribute officially to the programme as a sign of its commitment to combat racism. It has not yet done so.

Many see the Programme to Combat Racism as a prophetic sign of the willingness of the Church to take risks for the sake of the Gospel. To be ready to stand alongside the oppressed and the exploited may be to jeopardize its good name, but it is the price to be paid in the cause of the kingdom of God in an evil world. Others are not so sure.

QUESTIONS FOR DISCUSSION

1. Britain is now a multi-racial country. Do you see this as a privilege or a threat?

2. It has been said that church-goers are no less racist than those who do not claim to be religious. Do you think this is a fair judgement? What should be the Christian attitude to questions of race and nationality, and why?

3. Christians have to take a share of the blame for anti-semitism all down the ages, and therefore have a special duty to oppose it wherever it is seen to persist. What can the local church do to help a better understanding between Jews and Christians?

4. The Archbishop of Canterbury has said that to meet with members of other (non-Christian) faiths is to give us a fresh perspective on our own, and a new respect for other religious traditions. From your own experience (if any) do you think this is true?

5. What responsibility has the local church (or council of churches) for improving community and race relations in your area? How can it be done?

6. Some people have described the present United Kingdom immigration laws as racist. If this is true, is there any way you can suggest by which this criticism can be remedied, bearing in mind that every country must have some control of immigration?

Notes

1. *Racial Attitudes in Britain*, page 2.

2. Revelation 7.9.
3. *Theology and Racism,* page 11.
4. Quoted in *The Common Bond,* page 4.
5. *Racial Attitudes in Britain,* page 13.
6. For further information write to the Commission for Racial Equality, 10/12 Allington Street, London SW1E 5EH.
7. For further information write to the Community and Race Relations Unit. British Council of Churches, 2 Eaton Gate, London SW1W 9BL.
8. Quoted in *Sheep and Goats,* page 11.
9 *Racial Attitudes in Britain,* page 5.
10. *The Church of England and Racism,* pp. 17–19.

For Further Reading
Racial Attitudes in Britain: The Way Forward, The Archbishop of Canterbury (CIO Publishing)
People, Churches, and Multi-Racial Projects, Tony Holden (The Methodist Church Division of Social Responsibility)
Theology and Racism I (Church of England Board for Social Responsibility)
The Common Bond, Christians and Jews: The right approach to Catholic Jewish Relations (CMO Publications, Ashstead Lane, Godalming, Surrey GU7 1ST)
The Church of England and Racism. The Leicester Consultation 1981 (The Church of England Board for Social Responsibility)
Thinking the Unthinkable and Saying the Unsayable A comment from the British Council of Churches Community and Race Relations Unit.
The Closed Door. A Christian Critique of Britain's Immigration Policies, Keith Jenkins (British Council of Churches)

Sheep and Goats: British Nationality Law and its effects,
Anne Owers (CIO Publishing)
Understanding Race A study pack for local churches
published by the Board for Social Responsibility,
Church House, Dean's Yard, London SW1P 3NZ

5. QUESTIONS ABOUT WORK AND UNEMPLOYMENT

Work and the workless

Parents do not necessarily expect their offspring to be top of the form. They are satisfied if John's end of term report announced that 'he has worked well'. Traditional Christian teaching sets a high store on hard work. This is thought to be one of the fundamentals of education. Victorians, whose morality we are now supposed to admire, even thought that if work was not only hard but unpleasant it was 'even better for you'. The public school system was founded on this belief which is sometimes called 'the protestant ethic'. But what has this conventional morality to say to a society in which nearly four million people are denied the opportunity to work, and many boys and girls leaving school go straight from the classroom to the dole queue? Nearly half those who cannot find a job have been out of work for over a year. Particularly badly hit are black people, handicapped people and ex-offenders. They are in the 'hard to find work' category. All this represents a huge cost to the nation; £10,000 million in lost production and services; £1,000 million in social security benefits and loss of National Insurance and tax payments.

But more important than the financial loss is the cost borne by the unemployed themselves and the communities in which they live. A twenty-four-year-old unemployed man wrote:

> 'I feel like a totally rejected useless burden on society, despite the fact that my greatest desire is to gain useful employment.'

As the period of being out of work lengthens, there is an increasing inability to plan for or look into the future. The unemployed often try to hide from public view what they are really feeling inside. The desire to retreat from everyday contacts brings an irritability and failure of nerve which can have a detrimental effect on marriage and family life. The divorce rate among the unemployed, and especially the unskilled, is double the national average. A Government report on social trends recently revealed that forty-three per cent of unemployed men between the ages of twenty-five and forty-four are heavy drinkers compared with only twenty-eight per cent at work in the same age group. General practitioners note an increased incidence of heart disease, mental illness, and chronic sickness among the unemployed. Lord Scarman has noted that in Brixton where three-quarters of black men are unemployed there has been a sharp increase in burglaries. He sees a clear link between these two facts.

In areas of high unemployment there is a visible deterioration in the quality of life in the community. Less money is available for public services and social amenities. Property is in need of repair, or renovation. Street corner shops and small businesses relying on local custom are forced to close. In those parts of the country where a high proportion of the population is still in employment and doing nicely there is scant recognition of the misery and degradation suffered in those places where a substantial number have been forced to join the dole queue with no immediate prospect that the situation will improve. How and when can a solution be found?

The Conservative party under Margaret Thatcher's leadership believes that people must get on with the business of making a living with the minimum government interference. Competition increases efficiency. Efficiency creates wealth and brings back employment. In time market forces will create the prosperity we hope for. Others claim that this policy can be seen not to have succeeded. Only massive public expenditure will create jobs and restore national morale. Others offer various mixes of the two recipes. The party in power always says 'Give us time and you will see that our policies work'. The parties not in power always say 'Put us into Government and in due time there will be full employment'. The Christian religion offers no miracle cure for our present ills. The problems will not be solved 'at a stroke' whoever is in power. But Christians are urged to take the political and economic life of the country seriously, and to see this as one of the obligations of discipleship. We must do our best to understand what solutions the various parties have on offer. We have to ask what are the human and moral values upon which policy is based. We must, if we feel strongly, join with others (not necessarily Christians) to promote the policies which in our judgement correspond most closely to the Christian conscience.

The future of work

All political programmes claiming to offer a complete

solution of the unemployment problem have to be viewed with caution. Modern advances in technology, especially in the field of electronics, suggest a future in which the familar patterns of work and leisure will disappear and full employment (in the old sense) will never return. We are already being made aware of the labour-saving revolution which awaits us. Soon electronic check-outs at supermarkets will make human cashiers redundant and link automatic stock control and recording systems which will dispense with most of the 'behind-the-scenes workers' in big stores. In motor factories a whole vehicle will be welded together in a few minutes. Farmers will use electronically controlled tractors with no need for a man in the cab. Electronic technology is already revolutionizing banking, telephone systems, secretarial work, medical diagnosis. Information storage systems will add speed and efficiency to work in police stations and libraries, cutting manpower in those and similar areas. These things are beginning to happen. Science fiction is becoming fact. Precisely what changes will all this bring to the old patterns of work and leisure is debatable. But there is no doubt that the changes will be far-reaching, affecting the lives of us all.

What are the probabilities? There will be less full-time paid employment available. It is predicted that in twenty-five years' time it will require only a quarter of the present labour force to supply society with all its material needs such as food, clothing, housing and transport. This will mean much earlier retirement for most people. It may mean that young people will have to start full paid employment at a later age. Perhaps the sixteen- to eighteen-year-olds will be moved from the labour market altogether. A decline in employment in manufacturing industries may result in an increase in the service sector—office workers, telecommunication and postal services, the distributive and retail trades. It may mean that more men and women will be released from the old industries to work in those areas where robots cannot replace human skills—medical care, community and social work, education, art, drama, music and recreational services. Much routine, dangerous and dirty work may disappear. There may be far greater scope for part-time work, providing more leisure for political and social involvement in the community, and development of leisure-time activities and skills. Husbands and wives may be able to enjoy an equal share of time working outside the home and domestic involvement with house and children. If these things happen, will the life of most men and women be happier and more fulfilled, or will time hang on their hands and boredom become endemic? This raises great questions about the future of education. It will have to be seen to be as much concerned with preparation for leisure as for work. And this raises basic questions about the meaning of life, and the place of work and leisure within it. To this discussion the Christian faith has much to offer.

Work and religion

Both the Bible and the creeds open with a statement of belief in God as the Maker of heaven and earth. He is a working God. His work is creative. His work is good. Man is made in his image, and is commanded 'to till the garden and care for it'. This endows him with both the right and the duty to work. This is ratified by Jesus who was himself a worker on earth. In New Testament times a carpenter was the skilled and honoured industrial worker in the community making essential equipment for agriculture and for the home. When he told his disciples that his yoke was easy he may well have been recalling the claim that he and Joseph had made for the quality of their workmanship. 'The yokes which we make here will fit your animals well and comfortably.'[1] The Genesis story shows man to be a part of creation and yet to have been given authority to be a co-worker with God in the world. Work is necessary and God-given, but it is not always pleasant. Genesis depicts man as working by the sweat of his brow, and the 'sweat' is punishment for disobedience. In a world without sin all work would be entirely satisfactory and satisfying. Later writers, like the teacher writing school reports, see hard work as a good thing in itself. In the book of Proverbs the ant is held up as an example of profitable industry.[2] Many Old Testament characters are shown up as becoming prosperous through hard work, and this becomes the maxim of the Protestant work ethic. God helps those who help themselves. Work is also seen as an opportunity for people to strive together for the common good. The first murder in the Bible was the result of industrial rivalry where there should have been co-operation.[3] The Bible also acknowledges the economic necessity of work. Adam worked in the garden to provide for his wife and himself. But the prophets, such as Amos, insisted that if the products at work were not used for the relief of those in need, there must be strong condemnation.[4] Paul, describing how he earned his living as a tentmaker, wrote that a man does not deserve to eat if he refuses to work.[5]

These, and many other biblical references, can provide good basic criteria with which to assess present political and economic theory, and the way that plans should be made for the future. If large numbers of our people are denied the right to work, God's purpose for them is being frustrated and the system which creates the situation is sinful. If in the future many will not find the possibility of full-time and demanding work, in what other ways must society provide outlets for those creative and caring endeavours which are a sure mark that man is made in the image of his Maker? Christians should be ready to talk together about the options which the various political parties put before the nation for the lowering of the already unacceptably high rate of unemployment and to discuss what insights their faith can bring to this discussion. In most church congregations there are men and women with knowledge of the local employment situation, and the unemployed themselves have much to tell of their hopes and fears. In Telford a new rector was appointed. Soon after his arrival a parish conference was organized. He wanted an answer to the questions 'What are the major problems in this parish?' The conference decided that unemployment was much the most serious. A meeting of unemployed people was called together and in a short time an Enterprise, Resource and Social Centre was opened to serve the unemployed in the district.

Practical action for the unemployed

There is much that can be done here and now. It has been already discovered by groups of Christians in various parts of the country how they can show their concern not simply by talking or even praying, but by action. For example, a group of ministers (Anglican, Methodist, Presbyterian, Baptist) in a Yorkshire Council of Churches concluded a debate on unemployment by affirming that they would hold no more ecumenical services until they were united in ecumenical service for those in greatest need in their community. There are hundreds of practical schemes of caring in which local churches can be involved in their own neighbourhood. This usually means working with other churches and with secular bodies, perhaps with government help from the Manpower Services Commission. It is unwise for an enthusiastic congregation to launch into a plan of action without first asking many questions and doing careful research. What is the particular nature of the unemployment problem in our own district? What are the employment prospects for the next batch of school leavers? What is the immediate outlook for the future? What firms are in danger of closing down? What hopes are there for new kinds of employment? There are many points of contact where information can be gathered such as local trade unions and chambers of commerce. Other sources of relevant information are the managers of local Job Centres, the DHSS, the Manpower Services Commission, the diocesan Industrial Mission, and the Social Responsibility Boards of local diocese or church districts. Local Members of Parliament can help to fill in the picture. It is also necessary to discover how much the churches at the local and regional level have already been involved in discussion about action on unemployment. These preliminary enquiries may take time, but they are essential for any useful Christian involvement. This is the local equivalent of the 'language school' that a missionary has to undertake before going to take up missionary work overseas. Christian concern and action on behalf of the unemployed must not be seen as an 'optional extra' in the Christian life. It takes its place as an essential element in the mission to which Christ commits us in the place where we live.

An obvious need of many unemployed people (especially the younger ones) is to have a place to meet one another, and with those who can offer practical help and encouragement. But there are dangers that such centres can offer little else but temporary shelter. A Baptist group in Essex, considering the formation of a drop-in centre rejected a passive and negative approach and set out to develop a life style to meet the needs of those who felt bored, isolated and depressed. A group running a similar project in the North East asked whether the jobless, deprived of status, herded into dole queues, and fitted into numberless forms of bureaucracy, could really pioneer a new life ethic. They came to the conclusion that only the unemployed themselves could find an answer to that question.

'If the new lifestyle is to have any real meaning, it must be self-discovered, not something imposed from outside.'

The unemployed may need expert advice on welfare rights, or information on how to survive redundancy in middle age. But many of the best schemes are those which are run by the unemployed for the unemployed. In the information booklet *Action in Unemployment* published by Church Action with the Unemployed there are detailed descriptions of hundreds of projects in different parts of the country. There are many examples of training workshop projects in metal work, printing, woodwork, catering, electronics, computing, market gardening, needlework, office work, photography, toy making, even organ building. There are stories of derelict buildings being restored and of under-used church premises being put to fuller use. The Lincoln Diocesan Co-ordinating Unit has sponsored various projects in the diocese including construction of an adventure play-ground, the renovation of an old mill as a community centre, the conversion of a large house as a residential home for disabled people, building a Guide hut, rein-stating a barn and a cottage as a museum, repairing churches and village halls and much else. In spite of this impressive programme, the organizers complain of 'the lethargy among clergy and parishes in pro-viding projects'.

In Kettering, members of a prayer group drawn from four congregations launched an information and coffee bar centre for the unemployed, workshops for the establishing of small businesses, and a day centre for elderly, sick and handicapped people. They also set up a youth training scheme agency and a craft shop—all from a prayer meeting! In Truro, after con-sultation with others, the diocesan youth officer equipped a double decker bus as a mobile resource centre for the use of young unemployed. His advice was not to put into a building what you can put on wheels—especially in a rural area.

There are said to be a million small businesses in Britain. Existing ones could be expanded and new ones formed. In Bristol the New World Trust has con-verted an old factory site into fifty workshops for small businesses. In Greater London the Tower Hamlets Bridge Projects Trust offers training in set-ting up small businesses and provides a range of services such as basic book-keeping, publicity, obtain-ing insurance, finding premises, drawing up business plans and cash flow forecasting. Amongst the first clients to establish a viable business were a carpenter, a van driver, a wholesale supplier, a window cleaner, a puppet maker, a car sprayer and a boat builder. Many of these schemes are funded by the various temporary employment programmes initiated by the Manpower Services Commission. Robert Nind believes that the churches are ideally suited for this kind of initiative:

> 'because their long tradition of pastoral care and counselling enables them to enter into real relationships with a group of people in their prime of life who are having to pay the price for the security of the employed.'[6]

He warns that this must not be seen as a cheap way of getting repairs done to the Church Hall. The most important aspect of the Church's involvement with the unemployed is to build up a personal and perhaps lasting relationship of trust and hope in a society where those two qualities are sadly lacking.

> 'In partnership together during a period of a year's employment, providing that the Church does the job of management efficiently, staff and sponsors can share each other's deep feelings of struggle. But woe betide the church for which the end of employment means also the end of relationships, and woe betide the minister or church official whose relationship does not extend beyond the paternal pat on the back.'

The Church and the miners' strike

It was during the miners' strike in 1984–85 that the concern of the Church leaders for industrial questions came most forcibly to the attention of the public. The Churches were both praised and condemned for their involvement. Had they remained silent and inactive

106

they would have deserved far greater condemnation. Some politicians were particularly critical of the voice of the Churches at this time. Mr John Selwyn Gummer, a member of the Church of England General Synod, declared that the authority given to the bishops was episcopal not technical. 'They can no more pontificate on economics than the Pope could correct Galileo on physics.' But the Christian Church is concerned with the health of society, and the confrontation, division, violence and hardship created by the miners' strike were sure signs of sickness in our national life. The leaders of Church opinion had no particular skill to give clear guidance on the mechanics by which the strike could be ended, but they had responsibility as guardians of the faith of Jesus Christ to pronounce 'Thus saith the Lord' in this situation and to bring about, as far as they were able, his spirit of reconciliation and forgiveness. As one commentator put it, the bishops had one clear advantage over the protagonists, they did not have an entrenched position to defend nor did they have any particular face to lose.

Many attempts were made by the Churches acting together through the British Council of Churches and individually through their denominational leaders to bring the parties together in a spirit of reconciliation. They tried to impress both on the Coal Board, the National Union of Mineworkers and the Government the danger of either side attempting to achieve 'victory'. In this way they believed that only a serious stalemate would be reached, with the major problem unsolved. In the event, this forecast proved to be true. Early in the strike the President and General Secretary of the Baptist Union of Great Britain and Ireland wrote to the protagonists:

'We are ashamed of, and sickened by, the course of the present dispute between you. We recognise the immense difficulties involved in leading an industry through such a time of transition. We have paid careful attention to the arguments on both your sides, and have waited in vain for a creative lead from the Government.

As citizens and committed Christians we have reached the point when we must say to you: put aside your preoccupation with personal reputation and face-saving, stop looking over your shoulders for what your backers may say, and get together and stay there until you have come to some mutually accepted agreement.'

The Bishop of Sheffield in a letter to the *Sheffield Morning Telegraph* declared that whosoever was to blame in this dispute, truth itself was the first victim:

'I don't doubt that the leaders on each side are honest men who speak the truth to their friends, families and associates. But to us, the British public, they have offered such a mish-mash of accusations, half-truths and lies that it is simply impossible to get the truth at all.'

The Welsh Council of Churches together with the Roman Catholic Church in Wales put forward proposals for healing the strike, urging an independent inquiry. The British Council of Churches wrote to Mr Peter Walker, the responsible minister in the Cabinet, expressing the belief that 'no society should tolerate industrial and social dislocation on such a scale, or allow either side to demand total victory over the other'. They urged the Government to take a fresh initiative. Speaking in Derby Cathedral after a visit to a mining community, the Archbishop of Canterbury appealed to every Christian involved in the mining industry:

> 'Whether in management or union, or among the rank and file, to work together to consider how a new spirit of peace-making, the willingness to go the extra mile, can begin to work its way into our angry and divided communities, and draw the poison of bitter words.'

The Bishop of Durham, in his much publicized enthronement address, spoke of compromise as a Christian virtue and the only possibility. Would it help to cool the heat of the confrontation if the chairman of the Coal Board withdrew and the President of the National Union of Mineworkers climbed down from his absolutist demands:

> 'Without withdrawal and without climbing down, we are faced with several people determined to play God, and this gives us all hell.'

Christian spokesmen were ready to condemn the ugly violence at the picket line. The Archbishop of Canterbury spoke of the seeds of anger and mistrust which will bring a bitter harvest for both local communities and the nation at large.

> 'I have watched with dismay how some have taken the law into their own hands and unleashed violence. This lawless behaviour threatens one of our most precious national assets — good relations between hard-pressed police and the local communities. In our democratic country such desperate action cannot be justified.'

In an interview with *The Times*, the Archbishop spoke of the 'awful cancer of violence'. One of the major concerns of the representatives of the Churches was the damage which could be done to closely-knit mining communities by the strike itself, and the closing down of pits. This was dealt with appropriately by the Bishop of Durham as he assumed spiritual responsibility in a great mining diocese.

'No one concerned in this strike, and we all are concerned, must forget for one moment what it is like to be part of a community centred on a mine or works when that mine or works closes. It is death, depression and desolation.'

The Archbishop of Canterbury on a number of occasions pointed out the need to balance industrial efficiency with hope for the future:

'I have noted with disappointment how talk about economics and efficiency has not always been matched by an ability to feel the aspirations and emotions of miners and their families, or to communicate some vision of a hopeful future which can sustain our threatened communities.'

When the bishops were accused of interfering in the strike, the General Secretary of the National Union of Mineworkers told a newspaper reporter that 'he would be astonished if the Church leaders were not expressing concern about the hardship and poverty in the mining communities'. When the Trades Union Congress launched a miners' hardship fund, three of the four trustees were leading churchmen. The Moderator of the Free Church Council, Dr Howard Williams, explained that the fund was about need. 'It is not about merit or blame, it is not about reward or revenge. Quite simply it would be wrong to let hardship prevail'. The Bishop of Liverpool, another trustee, was photographed with a striking miner and his family reduced to selling the kitchen units and personal rings to raise cash to make both ends meet.

110

The third ecclesiastical trustee, the Archbishop of Liverpool (Monsignor Derek Worlock), pointed out that this was a hardship fund, not a fighting fund. 'We are concerned with the relief of hardship, and that is a proper role for Christians, and certainly for the Church.'

The Church of England Children's Society made a modest sum of money available through diocesan authorities for miners' children in need. Some critics accused the society of helping the strike, and it was found necessary to send out nine thousand letters of explanation. In a letter to Mr Peter Walker the British Council of Churches reminded him that throughout the British coalfields local churches felt they had a ministry to both sides of the dispute:

> 'There is no one Christian view on the rights and wrongs of the issue, but there is a common Christian commitment to minister to people in need and distress'.

Local churches organized communal meals and other aid to distressed miners' families. Some people who had no sympathy with the miners' case claimed to find support in Paul's severe dictum that a man who will not work should not eat. Most of the clergy working in the coalmining areas did not see it like that.

Even when both sides in the strike hardened their positions, and a solution seemed increasingly difficult to achieve, Church leaders were considering what lessons for the future could be learned from this tragedy.

Archbishop Derek Worlock spoke of 'the eleventh hour of our industrial era'. He claimed that the strike was:

> 'a symptom of the failure of our society to come

to terms with the post-industrial age, and should not be written off as the mere intransigence of two strong willed men.'

The Archbishop of Canterbury in an interview with *The Times* said:

'In a society where there is felt to be unfairness or in a society where things matter more than people, or where there is lack of meaning or responsibility or fulfilment to life, it comes out in the awful cancer of violence.'

In his enthronement sermon, the Bishop of Durham declared:

'There must be no victory for "us"—that is to say, society at large in our various groupings, who by our trends, tendencies and voting set up the sort of materialistic and consumer society we have. There will be no new hope for the future if all we get is the end of the strike and therefore, apparently, a quiet life again, and the assurance that "they" are dealing with these things. Our problems will not go away. We shall find hope only if more and more of us are prepared to face up to what is going on, what is wrong in it, and what might be brought out of it.'

The Bishop of Birmingham saw in the miners' strike a signal for a new national debate on priorities:

'We need to consider afresh as a nation, in the interests of justice, the distribution of gainful employment. We need to consider afresh the real nature of work, as against gainful employment. We need to consider the proper distribution of the national income between those who produce it and those who through no fault of their own cannot find gainful employment. We need to consider new goals for education in schools, training schemes, and further education, if a high percentage of those being educated are not going to be gainfully employed. We must have worthwhile goals for living, both for those who cannot find gainful employment and for those who can. What we need is a great national debate and a great educational process: these are urgently required.'

The dispute between the National Coal Board and the National Union of Miners, and the long damaging strike it caused, was not just another 'spot of bother' in the long catalogue of industrial disputes. It was a sign for those with 'eyes to see' both to Nation and Church. It was a call to the Nation to go into the future with its priorities right. It was a sign to the Church to cease being over-concerned with its own internal problems and to learn once again how to speak to the nation with the voice of prophecy: 'Thus saith the Lord'.

QUESTIONS FOR DISCUSSION

1. Discuss the fact and experience of high unemployment in the light of the Bible view of God's purpose for humanity. Would you agree that the present incidence of unemployment is not just an unfortunate fact of economic life, but a sin against God?

2. What practical action is taking place in your area to attempt to alleviate the worst effects of unemployment? Are the Churches involved? What more could be done?

3. Read the section above which describes the various interventions by church leaders and ecclesiastical bodies during the 1984–5 national miners' strike. Do you think that the statements and actions were an appropriate witness to the Gospel, or not the business of church leaders, or not outspoken enough? What lessons can the Church learn from this episode?

4. In the light of the Bishop of Birmingham's statement on page 112 discuss your view of the priorities which will be facing the nation as we move into a new technological age. Will the Gospel bring new insights and the Church find more opportunity for leadership in this changing situation?

Your discussion will be more down to earth if you can include a representative of management and/or the unions, and an expert on the future of technology in your discussions.

Notes
1. Matthew 11. 29–30.
2. Proverbs 2. 6–8.
3. Genesis 4. 8–16.
4. Amos 4. 1–3.
5. 2 Thessalonians 3. 10.
6. *Action on Unemployment*, page 5.

For Further Reading
Action on Unemployment. 100 projects with unemployed people (Church Action with the Unemployed, 146 Queen Victoria Street, London EC4V 4BY).

Further discussion literature on unemployment issues can be had from the Industrial Committee, Board for Social Responsibility, Church House, Dean's Yard, London SW1P 3NZ.

6. QUESTIONS ABOUT MAN AND NATURE

The changing countryside

A native returning to England after thirty years abroad would be surprised at the dramatic changes which have taken place in the familiar countryside. Downlands and meadows have disappeared under the plough. Ponds have been drained, hedges cut down. The conservation lobby is often accused of exaggeration, but there are many statistics to prove their point. Between 1937 and 1971 thirty-seven per cent of remaining downland in Wiltshire was ploughed up. There is a similar story in Hampshire and Sussex. Since the war about a quarter of our hedges have vanished, in some areas half of our ancient woodlands have disappeared. In some Scottish counties deciduous woods have declined by more than eighty per cent. Each year twenty-five thousand acres of wetland are drained. A huge proportion of herb-rich meadows and lowland heaths have been damaged or destroyed. Technology has turned farming into a highly efficient industry. Mechanization has displaced manpower and can operate at great speed in wide open spaces. New methods of animal husbandry and pest control have vastly increased food production. The countryside has become a factory, with new types of farm building,

116

tower silos and the ubiquitous electricity pylons giving an industrial character to the rural scene.

The technological changes in farming have brought great benefit both to the farmers and to the wider community with cheaper food. But they have been equally effective in putting the world of nature at great risk. Hedges, often of great antiquity, have been the natural habitat of large numbers of birds, insects, mammals and flowers. When hedgerows are destroyed to make larger fields, the future of these creatures is put in jeopardy. Technological change happens too fast for wild life to be able to adapt to the new situation. Many birds, butterflies and plants once familiar in our countryside are becoming rarer. Pesticides add to the tale of destruction. In a letter to *The Times*, Lord Melchett, David Bellamy and others gave a vivid account of what happened to an area in Essex, not far from Constable country, after it had been subjected to a 'ferocious mechanical operation', described by the local farmer as 'a trim and tidying up'. They described how boundary hedgerows of blackthorn, hawthorn, hazel and elder had been shaved to ground level. The same had happened to the hedge alongside a footpath which had been covered with wild roses, bramble, bryony and old man's beard. Gone were the scabious, wild violets and cowslips. Wide strips of hedgerow running alongside a ditch had been razed to the ground, denuded of wych elms, saplings, shrubs and undergrowth with the overall result that what was once rural farmland now looked more like a prairie. A stretch of disused railway line, a sanctuary for wildlife of all sorts, had had its young oaks torn out, had been levelled and put under the plough. Whilst the machines roared and whirred, Europe's grain mountain grew bigger.

This, they said, was not just topsy-turvy. It was an act of vandalism. If a man pulled down an eighteenth-century church on his land, he would be in trouble. Many of the hedgerows in our country are hundreds of years old. They asked how it was that the farmer is permitted to destroy a heritage he cannot replace. Food must be provided and the farmers must make a living, but this did not have to be at the expense of the English countryside and our native wildlife. It was, they declared, both brutal and irresponsible to anni-hilate our rural heritage.

It has been calculated that whilst the British envi-ronment of hedgerows and semi-natural meadows can support thirty-seven species of birds, twenty of mam-mals and seventeen of butterflies, the modern farm-ing environment can support only six species of bird, five of mammals and two of butterflies. Another calculation is that whilst twenty-four species of butter-fly can live on the old permanent pastures, grass leys do not provide a food plant for a single species. Dr David Goode, of the Nature Conservancy Council, has said that if current trends continue there is no doubt that many species of plants and animals will become extinct in Britain before the end of the century. Already the large blue butterfly and four species of dragonfly have been pronounced extinct in this country since the war, though attempts are now being made to re-introduce the butterfly.

Reverence for life

Albert Schweitzer once said that a man who is really ethical goes out of his way to avoid injuring anything living. Many people today are beginning to see the threat to our natural environment as a question of

118

morality. Organizations concerned with conservation such as the National Trust, the Royal Society for the Protection of Birds, the Council for the Preservation of Rural England and the Ramblers Association, all record increasing membership. National bodies have been established such as the Nature Conservancy Council and the Countryside Commission. There is a growing number of local amenity and conservation groups. Landowners, often depicted as the villains in this story, are showing awareness of their responsibility as custodians of the countryside. Both the National Farmers' Union and the Country Landowners' Association are putting conservation questions high on their agendas. There is indication that pressure groups are having an increasing influence on those who have the power to make decisions. The Environment Secretary upheld the attempt of a local council to stop a farmer uprooting forty-two acres of woodland in Kent, the home of nightingales and rare flowers. The Minister also imposed planning controls for the first time on a landowner who wanted to drain an important area of the Norfolk Broads. The Nature Conservancy Council, which is a government watchdog, is able to designate special sites of scientific interest for protection.

What should be the concern of the Christian in these matters? In an address to the Royal Society of Arts, Sir Ralph Verney declared 'We must have faith in a moral vision and the hope of moving towards an understanding of a true relationship between nature and society'. The Christian religion, with the witness of the Old and New Testaments, can provide that 'moral vision'. The Bible begins with the story of God creating the earth. The creeds speak of the Holy Spirit as 'the lord and giver of life'. John, in the opening of

119

his Gospel, describes Jesus Christ as the word 'through whom all things came to be, no single thing was created without him'. The thanksgiving prayer in the Church of England service of Holy Communion (ASB Rite A) expresses the same thought. Jesus is God's living Word 'through him you have created all things from the beginning'. Paul told the people in Corinth that 'the earth is the Lord's and everything in it'. All this means that the earth is not ours to do with as we like. God made it. It belongs to him. We are stewards and trustees. Because the world is part of God's creation it has value in its own right and not just because it is useful to us. It was here millions of years before man appeared on this planet. It will be here millions of years after man has vanished from earth. Man is part, but only part, of creation. He must approach it with reverence and awe and not in the spirit of exploitation and arrogance. Teilhard de Chardin has called nature the 'art of God'. To destroy the countryside is like destroying a Rembrandt painting or a medieval cathedral—only worse. God's purpose is working out in the complex interaction of natural life. If we obliterate a species or destroy a habitat, we may be doing irreparable damage to the evolutionary design of the Creator.

Professor Charles Raven, theologian and field naturalist, used to enjoy telling his students in Cambridge how Paul caught the vision of God at work in the processes of nature. 'The created universe waits in eager expectation, groaning in all its parts as if in the pains of childbirth.'[1] Was the great apostle, Charles Raven asked, anticipating the insights of the modern biologist as he explores the mysteries of evolution in which the hand of God can still be seen painstakingly at work in the natural world? If we look at nature and the world around us in the perspective of the Creator God still at work in the world, would we not be more shocked at the callous way in which we mar or destroy God's handiwork? Dr Anthony Russell, speaking at the Coventry Diocesan Synod, accused the Church itself of indifference and ignorance:

> 'The widespread concern for environmental and ecological issues which has been such a marked feature of recent years has had little impact on theological thought, and theologians have played only a small role in the debate.'

Because man can see the hand of God in nature, he needs access to the natural world and time to enjoy it. The appreciation and enjoyment of the world around fulfils a deep spiritual need. All down the ages, poets have testified to this. For Wordsworth the loveliness of the Wye Valley at Tintern enabled him 'to see into the life of things'. For William Blake, nature enabled him:

> To see the world in a grain of sand,
> And a heaven in a wild flower,
> Hold Infinity in the palm of your hand,
> And Eternity in an hour.

Conservationists are not demanding a luxury. They are pleading for a necessity. The longing to get close to nature is reflected in the huge popularity of wild life programmes on television. Each summer, crowds flock to well known 'beauty spots', though commercialization and the residue of Coca-Cola cans and crisp bags often spoils the very thing they have come to see. Those who want to get away from the crowds (as an increasing number of young people do) and hope to enjoy the 'bliss of solitude' are sometimes frustrated by farmers who have blocked ancient rights of way, or by the Ministry of Defence who claim large tracts of some of our finest countryside for military exercises. It is not only our duty as stewards of God's creation to preserve reasonable access to the countryside for all who wish to enjoy it. We have the responsibility to pass it on unspoilt to future generations. When we damage the natural world we not only rob ourselves. We are stealing from those who come after us.

Ethics and economics

The world of nature which we inhabit is not only there to be enjoyed. It is for us to use. The Genesis story of Creation tells us how God said to Adam and Eve:

> 'Be fruitful and increase, fill the earth and subdue it, rule over the fish of the sea, the birds of heaven and every living thing that moves upon the earth. I give you all plants that have seed everywhere on earth, and every tree bearing fruit which yields seeds; they shall be yours for food.'[2]

In the course of history human beings have not been able to feed themselves without destroying large numbers of plants and animals. The moral question is now to find the correct balance between the claims of man and the claims of nature. When the Bible says that God gave mankind authority to rule over nature for his own survival and well-being, to what extent did he intend man to exercise that rule? What price must nature pay for man's survival? A true ethic of stewardship must strike as good a balance as possible between these two claims. There are other balances also to be taken into consideration. The measures which conservationists urge may cost the farmer, or the taxpayer, tens of millions of pounds. Are the conservationists seeking to protect Nature for the benefit of the few at the expense of the majority? Is the benefit to posterity to have priority over those who have unsatisfied needs today? If hedges are not to be pulled down, wetlands not drained, forests not cut down, every acre of farm land not ploughed and sown, who is to bear the cost? The 1981 Wild Life and Countryside Act embraced the principle that farmers who were constrained from exploiting the full potential of their land should be recompensed from the public purse. Some have criticized this provision because it produced 'a bonanza for land agents and district valuers'. Sir Ralph Verney, a former chairman of the Nature Conservancy Council believes most strongly 'that conservation can only succeed by consent and must be an attitude rather than a legal commandment'. So he has opposed the payment of large sums of money to landowners to refrain from commercial activities which would be contrary to the interest of wild life conservation:

'Freedom to do what you like with your own is a very precious privilege of democracy, but it can only be justified if it is exercised responsibly with proper respect for the needs of the community.'

Professor D. K. Britton has lectured and written extensively on the economic and social aspects of modern agriculture. He believes that for the sake of the farming community money and morals have both to be taken seriously:

'It is at that moment when the scale of expected sacrifice tips against the expected benefit that the red light shows against further environmental improvement.... Schweitzer tried to establish an absolute moral principle; certain things are wrong and should not be done whatever the inconvenience or cost of their renunciation. The economist says; it all depends on the balance of gain and loss.'

In recent years there has been a growing conflict between conservationists and farmers. 'Farmer bashing' has become a popular pastime. Christians should work for a more positive and creative attitude, on both sides of the argument. Following Lord Melchett's letter to *The Times* (see page 117) the county chairman of the Stafford branch of the National Farmers' Union wrote to say how much the farmers in his own area were helping conservation in such ways as tree and hedge planting:

> 'No one is complacent but there is a growing number of farmers combining good farming with conservation. I honestly believe that the cause of nature conservation is best served by encouraging the many positive things going on rather than a constant stream of anti-farming propaganda.'

And Sir Ralph Verney has the same message of reconciliation:

> 'If conservation is to be by consent, as I believe it must, and if the ethic of stewardship is to be effectively deployed, great patience and sympathy must be painstakingly built up between conservationists and the farming community so that they understand each other's prides and prejudices and respect their motivations.'

May it not be an important task of the Church in the rural areas to initiate such a dialogue with 'patience and sympathy'?

Factory farming

One of the tests of civilized society is the way it treats

its animals. The most controversial aspect of modern farming is the application of technology to animal husbandry. The phrase 'factory farming' produces a shudder of distaste in a large section of the public. Yet it does not prevent most people from enjoying the products of this new rural industry. Hen batteries produce over ninety per cent of commercial egg supplies, and much of the relatively cheap pork and chicken available in the supermarkets is produced under highly controlled factory conditions.

Albert Schweitzer described compassion as the source of all ethics, and urged that this must embrace all living creatures and not limit itself to mankind. Today in animal farming, as in the growing of crops, economics plays a more important role than ethics. To those who absolutely oppose factory farming the case is clear. It goes against nature. Animals are tightly housed, given no bedding, standing on slat floors, confined to one environment in windowless blocks, reared and maintained in a constant background of drugs, antibiotics, vaccines, and artificial light. They are unable to turn, jump, move backwards or forwards, or take any kind of exercise. All this profoundly shocks those concerned with animal welfare. They accuse the farmers of callousness and cruelty. They are blamed for being much more interested in quick profits than in the well-being of the creatures in their care.

In turn the farmer accuses the welfarist of giving way to emotionalism based on an insufficient knowledge of the facts. They point out that farm animals under these conditions are safer and healthier than they would be in the natural state. They are not able to bully one another as they do when they range freely. They do not suffer from bad weather conditions. They have equal shares of food. Temperature, lighting, humidity, and ventilation are scientifically controlled to suit their well-being. They flourish better than those who have to live in normal open air conditions. They must be happy—look how healthy they are! Farmers are tempted to point out that a canary confined to a small cage in an old lady's sitting room or a pampered poodle in a town house with no freedom to roam, only able to go out on carefully supervised 'walkies', are in a far worse plight than the animals in their factory buildings.

Whatever arguments may be advanced in favour of intensive animal farming, many ordinary people (Christians among them) continue to register disquiet. Is this the way we ought to be treating our fellow creatures? But concern must not be based on feeling or ignorance. Dr W. B. Sainsbury, lecturer in animal health in the University of Cambridge, has said:

> 'I appreciate the concern of welfarists, but am often disappointed at their lack of knowledge of systems of animal husbandry and their extreme emotional attitude which has contributed to something of a confrontation between them and the agricultural scientists who to some extent take a rather extreme and sometimes arrogant attitude towards the genuine misgivings of the welfarists. You will note that I do not mention the attitude of the farmers. This is not an oversight, but because I think they are generally the most reasonable of all: the farmer and the stockman who lives closely to his animals rarely seems to me to be capable of cruelty, and I must say that I find some of the acts the welfarists ascribe to him nonsense.'

There is some evidence that mass production husbandry produces its own animal health problems. There are some experts who say that livestock thrive better in smaller units. Clearly more research needs to be done into ways of measuring stress in animals. These investigations need to be carefully monitored and evaluated.

Findings should be made public and not hidden in locked office files. Our consciences should remain alert to the ways we treat our fellow creatures. If, or when, there is cause for alarm, the Christian voice should be clearly heard. But our concern must be firmly based on facts. Guess-work or emotion are not enough.

Experiments on animals

In May 1985 the Government published a White Paper outlining proposed legislation for the control of scientific experiments on living animals. Most of the regulations in force dated back to the Cruelty to Animals Act of 1876. It was time that this difficult subject was given a new look. Not only have scientific investigations become much more sophisticated, but the work of various pressure groups has alerted the public to what may be happening behind the closed doors of research laboratories. With the development of alternatives to the testing of live animals the number of experiments in the United Kingdom has already fallen considerably in recent years. But the number of those which scientists still believe to be necessary continues to give rise to concern.

There is no doubt that great benefit to medical, veterinary and public health practice has been derived from laboratory tests on animals. It is generally agreed that these researches must continue. The ethical problem is to determine the degree of animal experiments allowable to advance medical knowledge. The legal problem is to formulate laws which are acceptable both to the research workers and to the public conscience—if it is possible that such a compromise can be reached. The 'animal rights' and 'animal liberation' movements believe that all experiments should be banned. Some of them have carried their protests to the extremes of doing criminal damage to property and even threatening and endangering the lives of those scientists of whose lawful activities they disapprove. 'They are', said one newspaper, 'so intoxicated by their cause that some of those in its service believe themselves to be absolved from the normal obligations of society and law.' These extremists do a disservice to the cause of animal welfare which needs to be examined with a much greater degree of intelligence and responsibility.

The Act of 1876 laid down that all experiments on living animals must only be performed under licence from the Home Secretary. In the first year after the Act became law, there were only three hundred surgical experiments. Today there are three and a half million each year. Eighty per cent of the licences issued are for experiments without the use of anaesthesia, though Sir Andrew Huxley, President of the Royal Society, has pointed out that such certificates are never granted for operative procedures more severe than are normally performed without anaesthesia on human beings. If the pain is severe and likely to endure, the animal must be killed painlessly forthwith, whether or not the main purpose of the operation has been achieved.

128

The Government's new proposals intend to restrict these regulations further. Two of the most controversial tests are to be phased out altogether. One is the irritant test which involves putting drops in the eyes of rabbits. The other is the toxicity test to measure the amount of poisonous material that can be fed to an animal before it proves fatal. Fifty per cent of those who undergo this test die. The licences issued by the Home Office will be much more rigid. The competence of the person authorized to make the experiment will be examined more closely. The nature of the proposed test will be more carefully investigated. Is it really scientifically necessary? Could the same experiment be done without the use of animals? What is the balance between the degree of pain involved and the benefit expected to be derived from the experiment? Special authority would be needed for experiments on dogs, cats, horses and monkeys. All animals used for research must come from registered breeding and supply establishments. The use of stray dogs and cats would be prohibited.

For some of these proposals did not go far enough. The British Union for the Abolition of Vivisection called them a confidence trick. The Animals Rights group called them a vivisectionist's charter. But many of the more moderate animal welfare organizations welcomed these proposals as clearly designed to reduce suffering, and as imposing new controls over the number and nature of experiments. The Minister of State at the Home Office told the Royal Society of Medicine:

'Most people do not want animal experiments to be stopped. They want the purpose of the work to be rigorously scrutinized, and the pain and suffering kept to a minimum.'

129

The former Dean of Westminster (Dr Edward Carpenter) led a deputation from the Christian Consultative Council for the Welfare of Animals to the Home Office to meet the Minister of State. They had two major anxieties to discuss: the degree of pain inflicted on unanaesthetized animals and the need for public accountability on the part of those who authorize and carry out these experiments.

Some Christians will continue to take the extreme view believing that vivisection is wicked, and therefore there is nothing more to be discussed. Others (probably the majority) want to see guidelines as defined by Dr Carpenter strictly observed. Pain and distress should be minimized and only inflicted when there is no possibility of an alternative procedure. The degree of pain and stress caused and the number of animals involved must bear a reasonable relationship to the importance of the objective in view. And the law should make clear, and the public be fully informed, of what is permitted and how it is being implemented.

When in Genesis God tells Adam that he must 'rule over the fish of the sea, the birds of the heaven and every living thing that moves upon earth' does this give man permission to experiment on animals for the undoubted benefit it may bring to both human and animal health? In the light of the spectacular progress in conquering disease which has already been achieved through such experiments, many people will be convinced that the answer is 'Yes'. Some will say 'No'. For others the question remains impossible to answer.

QUESTIONS FOR DISCUSSION

1. What arguments can be derived from the Bible in support of the conservationists who wish to protect the countryside from damage done to it by farmers, property developers, road builders, traffic and tourists? Does man's stewardship of nature receive much attention in the teaching given in the churches today?

2. If the development of the countryside is to be controlled, and the world of nature protected, should this be done by passing restrictive laws, or by the power of public opinion stimulated by pressure groups? What role has the Church to play in these matters?

3. The use of the land both for the production of food and for giving people refreshment and recreation often gives rise to a conflict between economics and ethics. Has the Christian a responsibility to take the economic argument as seriously as the ethical one?

4. Modern intensive farming methods have succeeded in making food cheaper and more readily available for everyone. The prohibition of factory farm methods might result in considerable price rises. Has the man who has a conscientious objection to factory farming methods the right to insist that other people, as well as himself, pay more for their food?

5. It is generally accepted that great benefits to medi-

cal, veterinary and public health practice have been gained from laboratory tests on animals. If these tests are not to be abolished altogether, how can a balance be achieved between the needs of scientific research beneficial to mankind, and the welfare of the animals involved in such experiments?

Notes
1. Romans 8.22.
2. Genesis 1. 28–30.

For further information you should talk to members of the local farming community and conservation societies. The Arthur Rank Centre at the National Agricultural Centre, Stoneleigh, Kenilworth, Warwickshire produces valuable material and courses on Christian responsibility to the natural world.

7. QUESTIONS ABOUT RELIGION AND POLITICS

'Meddling with politics'

In October 1984 in the middle of the national strike in the coal industry, the Archbishop of Canterbury was interviewed by *The Times*. In his conversation, which occupied a whole page of the newspaper, Dr Runcie spoke of the situation facing the nation and called for a new spirit of reconciliation. He had criticisms to make both of the conduct of the strikers with the violence at the pit heads and at the stubborness of the Government and the National Coal Board in refusing to seek some kind of compromise. In the days following the publication of this interview there was an outcry from many politicians accusing the Archbishop of meddling with politics and not sticking to his own job as a 'spiritual leader'.

One Member of Parliament called him 'a mindless muddled old man, naïve and foolish, who peddled Scargillism'. Another said, 'The Archbishop should have to eat coke in public as a penance. Dr Runcie should read in the New Testament to see how Christ avoided political judgements.' A third declared, 'Political disputes should be left to Parliament until the bishops have resolved their own differences about the Virgin birth'. These intemperate comments came from those who resented apparent criticisms from a church leader of the government which they supported. Had he focused his criticisms on the opposition, their comments might not have been so vociferous. They might even have commended the Archbishop for his good sense! This is all part of a growing unease voiced by many people in this country in recent years that the Church is becoming 'too political'. Not only Members of Parliament but writers to the correspondence columns in the national and church press have taken up the same theme. Many would agree with Mr Patrick Jenkin when he said in the course of a television discussion:

> 'The Church's primary role must be a spiritual one. I say this as a member of the Anglican Church. The churches are there to help us work out our own salvation according to Christ's interpretation of life.'

He added that it was not the job of the Church to enter into what he called 'the dusty arena' of politics. But is this a correct interpretation of the witness of the Bible?

At the heart of the teaching of the Old Testament is the Covenant between God and his people. At the heart of the teaching of Jesus is his proclamation of the Kingdom of God. Both Covenant and Kingdom are concerned with individual faith and corporate responsibility. Both involve spiritual life and social responsibility. In neither Kingdom nor Covenant can the idea of politics be excluded because this is the way we organize our life together for the benefit of the 'good life' of all, and for the protection of those who are most at risk. It is fascinating to study the Law books of the Jewish people in the Old Testament

(Leviticus, Numbers, Deuteronomy) and see how they worked out their covenant relationship with God in the organization of their life together as a nation. In those pages you will find laws regulating hygiene and health, sex, marriage and family life, responsible welfare for the poor and needy, the protection of the elderly, the deaf and the dumb, the treatment of aliens, rules about litigation and going to war, laws about property rights, fair trading, agricultural policy, industrial safety and nature conservancy. There is not a modern government department nor local authority office whose sphere of interest is not to be found in these books of the Old Testament. And all this is seen not only in the context of responsibility to neighbour but also of allegiance to God. Here spirituality and politics are part and parcel of the same religious response.

The prophets of the Old Testament testify to the same vision. Amos compares the emphasis put on 'spiritual things' such as ritual and ceremonial in worship with the neglect and exploitation of the poor. To him worship which is not matched with social responsibility is not true religion. Isaiah, surveying the frustration of Middle East politics, speaks powerfully of God's judgement on the nations of the world, and makes a plea for a new international order. Those who say that the Church should not concern itself with politics have clearly not understood the witness of the Law and the Prophets in the writings of the Old Testament.

The Kingdom of God

When we turn to the New Testament we see how central to the teaching of Jesus was the concept of the Kingdom of God. He taught his followers to pray for the coming of that Kingdom *on earth*. What does this mean? It means the coming of that time when God's will both for the individual and for the communities to which they belong will be fully realized. Men and women will have learned how to love God with all their heart, mind, soul and strength, and their neighbours as themselves. In a powerful parable he put flesh and blood on the idea of neighbourly love. It means feeding the hungry, giving drink to the thirsty, hospitality to the stranger, clothing the naked, relieving the sick, concern for the prisoner.[1] In the sophisticated and complex world of today, loving our neighbour locally, nationally, and internationally inevitably involves political action. There is no other way. The Christian faith teaches us the motives and dimensions of political involvement. Because Christianity declares that God is creator and ruler of the whole of life, the Christian cannot confine his interest to those things which are popularly labelled 'spiritual' or 'religious'. Because Christianity declares that Christ died for the sins of the whole world, the Christian's concern must embrace all nations, races and ideologies. Because Jesus himself claimed that he came to earth 'as a servant', the Christian knows that power (including political power) is given in order to serve the well-being of others and not to dominate them. Because Jesus is the pattern of what man should be, the Christian knows that the purpose of life, both personal and political, is to enable all people to enjoy a full humanity. Because Jesus came to give the new commandment to love one another, Christians know that at the centrepoint of all social and political life must be love for others with his kind of loving. In our modern world which some have called a global village, my neighbour is anyone to whose need I can

136

in some way bring compassion. This is the Kingdom of God for which we pray and of which the Church is an instrument. It stands as a challenge to any social or political order yet devised by man. It offers the hope of change by pointing to a future which is not of our making but in the hands of God. Edward Schille-beeckx, the Dutch Dominican theologian, sums it up:

'The Kingdom of God is a new relationship of man to God, and its tangible and visible sign is a new kind of liberating relationship between human beings in a peaceful and reconciled society.'[2]

The Christian and the ballot box

As a citizen in a democracy the Christian has the same responsibility as anyone else. He should take an intelligent interest in the political scene and cast his vote in accordance with his conscience. His faith will not give him clear guidance to vote for a particular party. No party can claim to be always right, and it is dangerous for any party to claim to be more Christian than the others. Parliamentary debates sometimes give the impression that speakers consider their own side to be entirely right and the other side entirely wrong. But much of the party political game is shadow boxing. Some of it is silly. There are Christians of deep religious conviction on both sides of the House. They know that their party sometimes gets it wrong, though it is not deemed politically prudent to admit it too loudly. But the Christian voter has a particular opportunity of testing the values of his own faith and witnessing to others by the way he approaches his political responsibility and by the questions he asks of those who solicit his support.

Before the General Election of 1983 the British Council of Churches issued a guide to the sort of questions Christians should ask prospective candidates and doorstep canvassers. Among the suggested questions were:

Do you believe that it is desirable to institute a level of minimum income in Britain?

Do you accept that a return to full employment as we have known it in recent decades is impossible during the lifetime of the next Parliament?

Do you agree that all public policies should be formed so as to encourage lasting marriages and stable family life?

Are you committed to the availability of the best possible health care to the whole community on the basis of need rather than on the ability to pay?

What steps would your party take to ensure that both the quality and quantity of our overseas aid programme be rapidly improved?

Such questions would encourage the candidates to express their political philosophy, reveal their aims and basic ethical stance and raise important and sometimes neglected issues. They would help to highlight the real difference between the parties, and indicate the sort of priorities a Christian would hope to find in a political programme worth supporting, such as poverty, unemployment, marriage, health and the responsibility of support for the developing world.

Most Christians (though not all) would agree that their religious faith must have some influence on their personal political choices. But when the Church as an institution begins to make political pronouncements or becomes involved in political action, there is widespread anxiety. As we have seen, the teaching of the Bible suggests that such anxiety is unfounded. What are the possibilities and dangers of such explicit involvement? Locally the churches, perhaps through their Council of Churches, may feel compelled to make representations to the local authority on some public matter involving moral principle. They may believe it right to join with others in pressure groups, demonstrations or campaigns on such questions as welfare rights, racial discrimination, unemployment or education. In some areas councillors and chief officers try to take to themselves exclusive responsibility for community welfare and are often suspicious of voluntary organizations (including the Churches) and discourage any private initiative. In some city and town councils the ruling party leaders are so concerned with party advantage that forwarding the well-being of the whole community takes second place. Public officials are sometimes tempted to use their powers to act as petty autocrats appearing to treat those who come to them for advice or assistance (which they are paid to give) as potential nuisances. Participation is an essential element in a healthy democratic society. Ordinary citizens should demand the right to make a positive contribution to the decision-making process. But as Margaret Simey has pointed out:

'What we have now in effect is not government by consent but government by remote control. Today for many people significant parts of their lives are dominated by decisions taken by others on their behalf against which they feel it is useless to protest.'[3]

139

Risk and compromise

In South Africa, Latin America and Poland the Church sees an essential part of its task to give a voice to those who otherwise cannot be heard. Even in the freedom of a democratic society such as in Great Britain there are those who feel powerless to influence those who claim to have authority over their lives. Particularly in the inner areas of our great industrial cities, where so many human problems are concentrated, the Church is called to stand alongside the poor. To some this is seen as 'meddling in politics'. But many Christians know that not to do this would be to betray the Gospel entrusted to them.

The publication in December 1985 of *Faith in the City*, the report of the Archbishop of Canterbury's Commission on Urban Priority Areas received a mixed reception. In more than 300 pages, it discusses problems of poverty, unemployment, housing, health, social and community work, education, law and order in the inner cities. It has criticisms to make both of church strategy and political priorities. The Church of England and the Government are examined in the light of the Gospel. It gives praise to both Church and Parliament when that is due. But it is also severely critical of both.

Those who object to the Church 'meddling in politics' were quick to dismiss the report, even before they could have had time to read it with care. One Minister is said to have described it as 'pure Marxist theology' — whatever that means! Another MP said it was further evidence that the Church of England was 'run by a load of communist clerics'. Another immediately denigrated it as 'out of date, out of time, out of touch and unwanted'. Yet there is already

140

evidence that with the passing of time *Faith in the City* will take its place among the major documents of twentieth century Church life in Britain. Some of its conclusions may prove to have been misguided and some of its theology open to question. But the debate it has initiated inside and outside ecclesiastical circles is likely to be seen increasingly to be of major importance. This is precisely the way in which the Church must attempt to serve both the nation it is called to serve and the Gospel it is committed to proclaim.

Both on the international scale and in the local church, to express active compassion in political terms is to court the danger of compromise and risk. Action taken in all good faith may eventually prove to have been mistaken. Pronouncements which are made, even after the most painstaking thought, may sound ambiguous. Sometimes church spokesmen may seem to be jumping on the bandwagon following what Paul Rowntree Clifford has called the prevailing fashion of secular intelligentsia rather than the Gospel itself. Statements and action which are fully justified by Christian conscience may nevertheless cause distress to some devout and faithful church members whilst rejoicing the hearts of many outside the churches hoping for a lead from them. The Church, both locally and on the wider stage, must be prepared to take risks if it is to try to witness faithfully to the implications of the Gospel of Jesus Christ in the complexities of the modern world. The only alternative is to keep silent and retreat into our own little ecclesiastical world, comforting one another, but utterly failing in our evangelistic task.

When the World Council of Churches met in Vancouver in 1983 many people in Britain were distressed by the radical tone of some of the statements which emerged. These were strongly influenced by the insistent voices of Christians from the new third world countries in Africa, Latin America and Asia. They said things of little comfort to the traditional Churches of the west, and there were hostile comments in the British press accusing the Council of being quite out of touch with the 'ordinary Christian' in the pew. Canon Paul Oestreicher, of the British Council of Churches expressed the dilemma:

'The danger is not that the World Council of Churches is out of touch with the ordinary Christian. It usually speaks only too eloquently for the world's ordinary Christians most of whom are neither well-fed, white, nor western. That is why the average British churchgoer is so disconcerted. We cannot easily get used to being one of the world's minorities. I can attest to this personally. At home my views are held to be left wing. Abroad, more often than not, I find myself somewhere to the right of centre. The World Council of Churches' problem is that it is very close to the global centre, yet its task is to reflect Jesus its Lord and not necessarily its membership. The Church has no real choice. The world's agenda must be its own agenda. But on God's terms. Woe to the Church which avoids the social, economic and political issues of its time. Only in facing political conflict can politics be transcended and healing brought to the world.'

In this book we have been looking at some of the questions for today which profoundly concern the quality of life for all of us. Marriage and the family, control over life and death, law and order, employment and unemployment, race and nationalism, and

142

the preservation of our environment. In each of these areas we have to make personal decisions. But each also is the concern of government. How can the laws they make strengthen what is good in our society, and diminish what is evil? The politicians we elect are responsible to us for the decisions they reach. But we are responsible to them for giving what guidance, criticism and support we can. In that process of give and take between the governors and the governed, the Church of Jesus Christ has a prophetic role to play.

QUESTIONS FOR DISCUSSION

1. What fears lie behind the often-heard criticism that 'the Churches today are meddling too much in politics'?

2. What support does the Bible give to the view that Christianity is concerned with the structures of society and not just with personal morality?

3. What are the arguments for and against having a specifically Christian political party in Parliament?

4. Why are the questions addressed to parliamentary candidates on page 138 the particular concern of Christians? Can you suggest other questions which could be added to the list?

5. Are there occasions when the Church should make specific statements or take direct action concerning policies advanced by the Government or other

parties? Can you give examples particularly from the areas of concern discussed in this book?

In discussing these questions it would obviously be a help to involve politicians and local councillors of different political persuasions.

Notes
1. Matthew 25. 31–46.
2. *God Among Us*, Edward Schillebeeckx, page 107 (SCM Press).
3. *Government by Consent*, page 5.

For Further Reading
Politics and the Christian View, Paul Rowntree Clifford (SCM Press)
Bias to the Poor, David Sheppard (Hodder and Stoughton)
Faith in the City. The report of the Archbishop of Canterbury's Commission on Urban Priority Areas (Church House Publishing)
A Christian Approach to the Welfare State, Stephen Orchard (British Council of Churches)